Praise

Who is God Now?
Hope in God after Betrayal

When Robin Wilson experienced her own personal "D-Day" due to her husband's infidelity, she armed herself with God's Word to fight courageously to save her marriage. Her book chronicles her journey through the highs and lows of remaining faithful to God's calling. A must read providing hope for those who have endured betrayal.

—Josh D. McDowell, author

***

I am pleased to recommend this book for those who love God and who find their hearts broken after sexual betrayal. *Who is God Now? Hope in God after Betrayal* is an honest look at the process of wrestling with and hanging onto God and faith after crushing disappointment and the grief of betrayal. Robin and Christy provide helpful suggestions for clinging to God as Robin was impacted by the betrayal of her husband. I love the vulnerability Robin shares as she leaned into her faith and relationship with God as she grieved, worked to determine what she needed, and ultimately grew in her love for her Savior while she worked to recover from her betrayal experience.

If you have been betrayed, you know how shattering that can be to every aspect of your life. This book will encourage you to stay connected (or to connect for the first time) to the God who knows and sees and loves you.

—**Barbara Steffens PhD,** retired counselor, founding president, Association of Partners of Sex Addicts Trauma Specialists *(APSATS),* co-author of *Your Sexually Addicted Spouse; How Partners Can Cope and Heal (Steffens & Means, 2009, 2021)*

***

It is refreshing what Robin and Christy have created for women facing the devastating pain of betrayal. *Who is God Now?* provides genuine hope for healing from betrayal. It also encourages the reader that soul restoration is possible no matter what happens in the relationship. I recommend this book to any woman who wants true healing, abiding peace, and counterintuitive joy that can only come through an honest journey with God.

—**Jonathan Daugherty**, founder at *Be Broken Ministries*

***

Looking for a book that feels like a heartfelt chat with an understanding friend? *Who is God Now?* by Robin Wilson is your perfect choice. Join Robin on a transformative journey from the wrenching pain of betrayal to a place of healing and invigorating hope. Her story is not just relatable; it's genuinely inspiring. Having traversed the depths of despair herself, Robin assures you that even amid the darkest moments, the radiant love of God perseveres.

What sets Robin apart is that she's not only empathetic but also has emerged stronger through her experience with MOF (Mighty Oaks Foundation). Now, she's extending that hard-earned wisdom to others who are seeking solace. So, if you're grappling with the aftermath of infidelity tearing your marriage apart, don't miss this gem. It's akin to a guiding flashlight, leading you toward a deeper connection with God and a renewed sense of self.

Believe me, as you close the final page, it'll feel as though you've just had a profound heart-to-heart with a compassionate and sage friend. *Who is God Now?* is that powerful and transformative.

—**Chad Robichaux,** founder of *Mighty Oaks Foundation* and bestselling author of *Saving Aziz*

***

Robin and Christy have created a work that every woman in this circumstance should grab hold of! I know too well our tendency is to put all future hope in our husband's change of heart. A profound antidote is to immerse oneself with His ancient, eternal truth for life-changing clarity that He is the Rock our hope should be anchored in. Robin and Christy's book does just that, guiding you to put your hope in the One that doesn't disappoint. Renewed joy, healing, and a deeper relationship with God are magnificent rewards.

—**Susan Allen,** founder, *Avenue for Women*

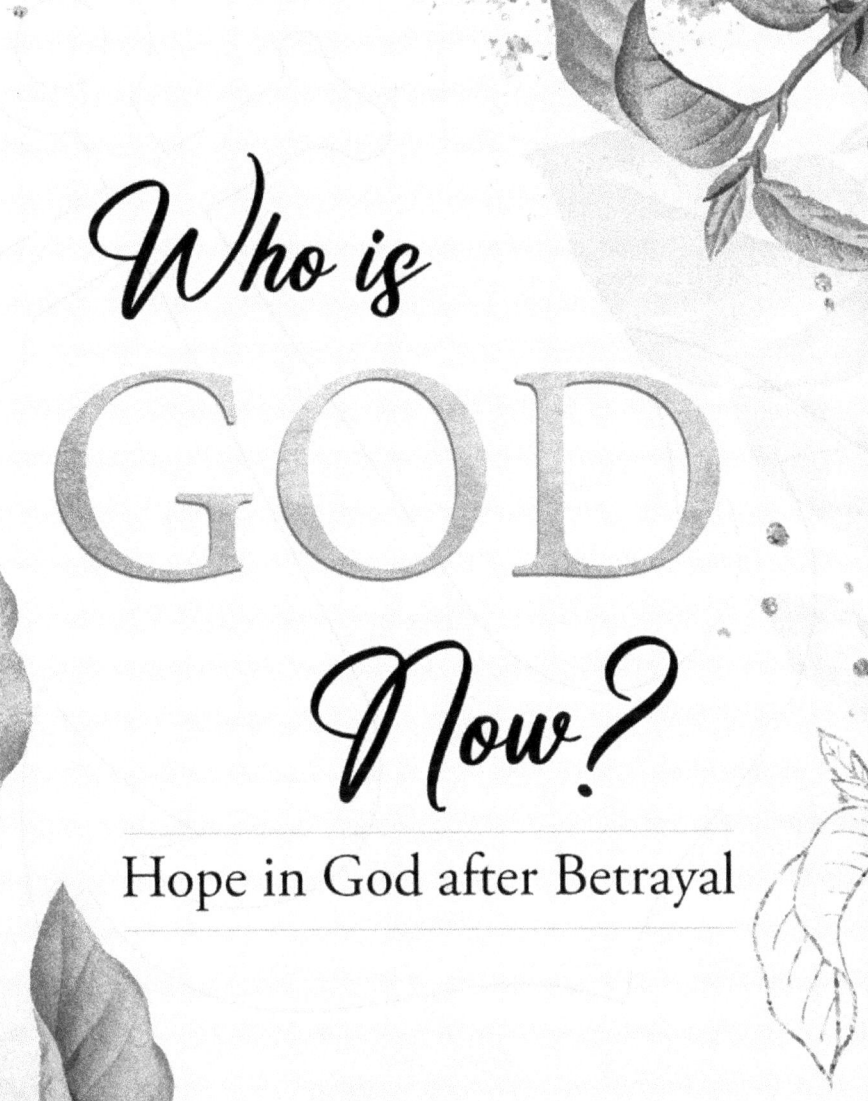

Who is GOD Now?

Hope in God after Betrayal

Robin Wilson
&
Christy Bottom

Published by KHARIS PUBLISHING, an imprint of
KHARIS MEDIA LLC.

Copyright © 2024 Robin Wilson and Christy Bottom

ISBN-13: 978-1-63746-261-4
ISBN-10: 1-63746-261-1
Library of Congress Control Number: 2024946494

All KHARIS PUBLISHING products are available at special quantity discounts for bulk purchase for sales promotions, premiums, fund-raising, and educational needs. For details, contact:
Kharis Media LLC
Tel: 1-630-909-3405
support@kharispublishing.com
www.kharispublishing.com

I wrote this book for Brandy, Jess, Christina, Leticia, Nena, DeeDee, Amanda, and every other beautiful soul who has found, or may find herself navigating the discovery of a betrayal and the journey that beckons. You are cherished.

Contents

Chapter 1

D-Day

Here you are, stuck in the turbulent backwash of someone else's sin, severely wounded by your husband, the person who made a covenant promise to love you until death. If you have been lied to, cheated on, abandoned, left out to dry—this book is for you. On days when your head starts spinning from anxiety or fear, this book will take you back to what we know (and hope you know or will know) to be true about God.

It's those truths about God—what's in His nature—that kept me grounded during my own recovery from marital betrayal. I've been where you are. I called it my "D-Day."

The Battle of Normandy, better known as D-Day, has been considered "the beginning of the end" of World War II. I researched D-Day and found there's not a straightforward answer for what the "D" in D-Day actually signifies. The D in my D-Day meant: disclosure, devastation, a delineation of before and after. The knowledge I received on that day threatened to destroy my marriage, my family, and my entire life. My D-Day was August 23, 2021, the day that changed everything.

First came the shock. The enormity of the betrayal hit me like a freight train, making me gasp for breath from the waves of realization of deceitfulness and hypocrisy.

Then the questions. How does a person go back to normal life on Monday? How do I answer when my coworker asks me, "How are you?" How do I pour my coffee with one hand while realizing the bitter cup I've been asked to drink with the other? Will life ever feel normal again?

Then reality.

This reality differs for each person. For some, it's the quick severing of a relationship. Others will hold on, perhaps in the interest of children or a million other reasons. Despite all best efforts, there may come a time when the healthier decision is to let go. Still others may find their loved one seeking forgiveness, repenting, and working towards restoration—a different, but nonetheless difficult journey to travel.

This is no easy process! Nor is there a timeline, potion to drink, or magic pill to swallow to make things better.

But WE CAN HAVE HOPE!

More important than the details of my story is what I discovered about God afterward. While my marriage at that point was as dead as the side part and skinny jean trends, my story didn't end there. On D-Day, I had a choice–just like you do. I could choose to give in, let this event overtake me and define the personal narrative of my life, or I could fall helplessly into the arms of Jesus. I could let Him use this event to mold me and grow me into a person after His own heart.

Maybe you're in that place of limbo, sensing something is very wrong, but not having any evidence to prove it. Do you get a feeling that you should follow your husband and then catch him in the act? Are there charges on the credit card statement that don't make any sense or disturbing websites on your computer's history? Do you two fight about how flirtatious he seems with waitresses or the babysitter? Maybe he's repentant. Maybe he's not. Maybe he's in prison. He could very well still be on that downward spiral of self-destruction. Perhaps your marriage is already over, and you're in a safer place now. Perhaps he's sitting beside you right now on the sofa.

Even if the relationship you're in seems hopeless and there's no possibility for repair, God's character is steadfast. When we look to Him, His character becomes our hope. Along my journey I sometimes found myself thinking, *I knew who God was before, but now that this has happened, who is God now? Where is He?*

The truth is, God hasn't changed. He is still truthful, even when people in our lives aren't. He is still gracious. And trustworthy. And loving. For all the reasons we first found ourselves in love with our merciful Savior, we can still praise Him! Hebrews 13:8 (NIV) gives us this promise: "Jesus Christ is the same yesterday and today and forever." Our flawed human relationships can never erase the perfection of God's character. We don't have to let them taint the way we view our relationship with God. God is beyond our own human understanding and heartbreaks. We would be wise to remember that His character does not change. When it feels like our lives are falling apart outwardly, it can be a constant struggle to keep these feelings of grace and hope in our hearts. This is why I've written this book.

You are not alone. The unfortunate reality is that far too many women are facing situations just like yours: feeling lonely and abandoned by the one who is supposed to love you the most. This book was written to point you to God and His Word, to remind you of God's overwhelming, incomprehensible love for you, and to encourage your soul to be quick to remember these truths.

My hope is that once you've centered yourself on who God is and how He sees you, you will be able to pass along this book—dog-eared, a little worn around the edges—to a dear friend who now needs the strength and encouragement in its pages. While I can't promise things will get better soon, I can promise you have a God who holds you in His hands, who walks with you now and always.

I chose Jesus, clung to Him. I found hope in God's promises and joy through a deeper relationship with the Lover of my soul. I experienced comfort and healing in His faithful arms. I hope you can experience that same hope, joy, comfort, and healing. None of these lessons came quickly or easily, and I recognize that the healing I've found in my marriage won't happen in all marriages.

My prayer, as you move into the next part of your story—whatever it may look like—is that you choose Jesus, too. As you lift your eyes to Him in this battle, He will meet you. You are a beloved daughter of the King; you are most certainly seen, heard, chosen, redeemed, and dearly loved.

The King of Kings is a disaster manager. A bomb was dropped into your life, obliterating it into millions of pieces of debris and shrapnel, but He will not retreat. He will accompany you as you sort through it. Today is a new kind of D-Day: Declaration Day. This is a day to declare that this explosion in your marriage will never separate you from the love of God, which is in Christ Jesus our Lord; a declaration that your story, when placed in God's hands, is a story of victory. The battle's already been won.

Prayer for Today

Lord, thank You that You are not done with my story. I'm confident that Your glory will be in full display as You walk with me through this mess. I'm eager to learn more about You and Your character. Let the dust and debris not be a distraction. It's my desire to see You clearly.

Chapter 2

He Loves Me Not, He Loves Me

"This is love: not that we loved God, but that he loved us and sent his Son as an atoning sacrifice for our sins."

1 John 4:10

After his betrayal, guilt and shame weighed heavily on my husband. (We'll call him "Will.") He tried to convince himself that he didn't love me, reasoning to himself that was the only way he could have made those choices and caused me such devastation. In fact, that's how it first came out: "I don't think I love you anymore." His sobs of grief said otherwise, but in the moment, the words blasted a hole in my soul.

One of the lies the Enemy wants you to believe after a betrayal is that you're not loved. If God loved you, He would never allow this to happen to you. The temptation to believe that was real for me. At the same time, my entire being—all of my faith—centered on the verse a lot of Christians memorize early in their faith journey: "For God so loved the world that he gave his one and only Son, that whoever believes in him shall not perish but have eternal life" (John 3:16). Without love, the gospel message is stripped of any meaning. If the man who claimed he'd love me until death did not really mean it, had God done the same? Didn't God know this was the most difficult trial of my life? If He really loved me, why would He allow this happen?

My son has a shirt from his Sunday school class that says, "If it's in the Bible, then it's 100% absolutely, positively true!" I've known since I was younger than my boy that everything in the Bible is true. I knew I had to stand firm on that fact.

The Bible confirms that God is immutable. If He never changes, His love is the same yesterday, today, and forever (Hebrews 13:8). Nothing in all of creation could take God's love away from me (Romans 8:38-39), and that included neither my, nor my husband's sin. I knew my life wouldn't be normal for a long time, so this had to be my constant. It was a truth I would come running back to again and again.

I wrote down every verse I could find about God's love for me on yellow sticky notes, then stuck them up on my bathroom mirror. (For some sticky note examples, turn to the back of this book.) Every day, I stared at them for six minutes while I dried my hair. For six short minutes, the sound of the dryer overcame the sound of the Enemy's voice. Sometimes I could only stare blankly at the yellow squares. Sometimes, I'd read the verses out loud, praising and thanking Him for His lavish love. Other days, I would desperately need to feel His love, praying that He would show me. These words were true. They are still true. They will be true, no matter how I feel about them or how much I am able to believe them. I was trying to cement them into my brain. If I could do that, how could I, or anyone else, ever convince me they weren't true?

God, in His divine omnipotence (unlimited power), was using the insufficiency of my husband's love to draw me to Himself. Nothing could have accomplished this purpose better. God Himself created love and is love (1 John 4:8). He is the love for which I had been desperately longing. I was beginning to grasp the truth that God's love is the only love that can truly satisfy my soul.

The truth of God's love also helped me fight my fears. After my husband left for work one day, I couldn't shake the feeling that he was never going to come home again.

My heart began beating faster and faster. My breath quickened. Was I imploding? What was I just working on? I tried to calm down, to focus, but I had to know if Will would come home that night. I felt abandoned and forsaken. I pictured my family in the future, now only four instead of five. I cried out to the Lord, "God give me peace!"

Finally, I thought to message my good friend and mentor. My hands trembled as I tried to text her. "I think I'm having an anxiety attack," I typed.

"Don't focus on the fear. Focus on Jesus' love," she responded. Then she quoted part of 1 John 4:18: "Perfect love casts out fear."

I ran upstairs to my bathroom. I started reading my sticky notes out loud:

He has loved me with an everlasting love.
God's love has been poured out into my heart through the Holy Spirit.
How priceless is Your unfailing love, O God.
Because of the Lord's great love, I am not consumed.
See how much my Father loves me, for He calls me His child.[1]

Because His love is an everlasting love, there is nothing you could do, say, or think that would make Him stop loving you. Nothing could make Him love you more or love you less. His love is not contingent on the state of your marriage, whether you choose divorce or reconciliation, or whether or not you doubt God's love for you. He loves you, even if you blame Him for your husband's affair or addiction. His love is not dependent on your behavior toward or responses to your husband. Every last one of us would be destined to Hell if God's love were determined by what we bring to the table. The greatest expression of love that the world has ever known is this:

---

[1] See Jeremiah 31:3; Romans 5:5; Psalm 36:7; Lamentations 3:22; 1 John 3:1

"While we were still sinners, Christ died for us" (Romans 5:8). He continues to love us, despite our sin, making His everlasting love even more awe-inspiring.

At the same time, God calls us to repentance and to a life of willing obedience to His commands. He gives us one such command in 1 John 4:7-8: "Dear friends, let us love one another, for love comes from God. Everyone who loves has been born of God and knows God. Whoever does not love does not know God, because God is love." God is the creator and giver of love. If we receive His love, His love can freely flow from us.

This command to love others was especially difficult when responding to my husband, who had acted so unlovingly towards me. Oh, how my flesh desired to come up with a way to repay him! I wanted to ruin his reputation and shame him at every opportunity.

One afternoon, shortly after D-Day, I had a conversation with a friend.

"Have you been praying for Will?" she asked.

The question made my pride swell and my nose squish up in disgust.

"No," I said.

She began to encourage me with something similar to the exhortation in 1 Peter 3:8: "Finally, all of you, be like-minded, be sympathetic, love one another, be compassionate and humble. Do not repay evil with evil or insult with insult. On the contrary, repay evil with blessing, because to this you were called so that you may inherit a blessing."

Could I show humility? Compassion? Love?

Let me emphasize that the above verse does not say we should excuse sin, deny it, enable it, or delay seeking safety for ourselves or our children. If your safety or that of your children is in jeopardy, get help.

Putting this verse into practice does not mean you are to have mandatory loving feelings toward your husband. It doesn't mean you have to be in your husband's presence at all. Sometimes one of the most loving things you can do is create distance from him, especially if he is being abusive or manipulative to you or your children.

You may be in a situation where your husband is not acknowledging that his behavior is a problem. Maybe he is blaming you for his sin. True love, as exemplified by God, never ignores sin. First Peter 3:8 never says love means you should passively stand by, watching your husband destroy your family without putting boundaries in place.

No matter how your husband is acting or what he is saying, you can choose to honor God with your responses. The verse is clear: love includes repaying evil with blessing. This goes against human nature, requiring the Holy Spirit's power to work through you. Romans 5:5b says, "God's love has been poured out into our hearts through the Holy Spirit." When the love gauge of your life is on full, spilling over with the abundance of God's love, that love pours out onto others. When you do things God's way, you are showing love to Him and inheriting the blessing promised in 1 Peter 3:8.

What does "repaying evil with blessing" look like after discovering infidelity in your marriage? This looks different for each of us. There are many situations in which it is safer and healthier to not have any contact or interaction with your husband. Talk with God and ask Him how you should navigate this. He knows that it's your heart's desire to honor Him in all of your responses.

For me, navigating this time meant overcoming my prideful thinking that I was a better person than Will. I started praying for him. I agreed to participate in the healing process by going to counseling sessions. I consciously made an effort not to use Will's sin as a weapon with which to wound him. I can't say I did this perfectly; it would have been completely impossible without the power of the Holy Spirit. The process required a clear understanding of what God's love had first done for me. For God so loved me, a wretched sinner, that He sacrificed His perfect Son to redeem me and bring me into eternal life with Him (John 3:16). God had given everything because of His love for me.

Jesus doesn't ask us to do anything that He's not willing to do. His words, written in Luke 6:27-28, command us: "But to you who are listening I say: Love your enemies, do good to those who hate you, bless those who curse you, pray for those who mistreat you." Jesus practices this throughout the Gospels. In Luke 23:34 He even prays, "Father, forgive them, for they do not know what they are doing," as He is actively dying. While I would never want to compare my own human experiences of forgiving other people with Jesus' experience of taking away the sins of the world, my point is that Jesus prayed, calling upon Abba Father to forgive those who were sinning against Him. With His example and the strength of the Holy Spirit to equip us, we can show love by praying for our husbands.

Prayer might not change our circumstances, but it will change us.

After I decided to try repaying the evil of Will's betrayal with blessing, I said a prayer through gritted teeth and with a bitter heart: "Lord help me to see Will the way You see him: as Your child, a child who is dearly loved by his Father." (I know some friends who have prayed a similar prayer and even looked at childhood photos of their husbands as they prayed. This helped them remember their husbands are God's children.)

This prayer of mine felt totally awkward. It didn't feel like what I wanted to say. How could I look at my husband like this? Eventually, as the Holy Spirit's comfort encircled me, my jaw unclenched. My heart started to soften. I started seeing Will more like God sees Him. My prayers became more frequent and more earnest. By praying in this way, I realized God was blessing me each day by relieving physical tension in my body and slowly releasing the bitterness in my heart. He didn't have to reward me for the obedience that He was worthy to receive, but He did so because of the generous love that He was pleased to share.

In His love, God relentlessly pursues a relationship with you. He desires to have your heart, to be loved in return, and to be trusted enough to have your faithful obedience. We will never be able to love Him back as perfectly as He loves us or as much as He deserves, but we can choose today to honor, obey, and trust Him. We can show love by choosing to be patient and kind towards our husbands. We can show them the love of God through our words and actions and our commitments to prayer. If during this season you find yourself doubting that you are loved, remember this: Nothing in all of the world can separate you from the love of God that is in Christ Jesus (Romans 8:39).

Prayer for Today

Lord, even though my husband's actions have caused me to feel unloved, Your love never fails. Nothing in the world can separate Your love from me. Erase my doubt. Empower me, through your Spirit, to love like You love.

Questions to Ponder

1. Meditate on the sticky love notes at the back of the book. Or perhaps you'd like to create your own. What do you discover about God's love as you do this? Which truths will you choose to cling to today?

2. God's love for you is endless, and it fills every void. His love never fails. When you feel unloved by your husband, read John 3:16 and replace "the world" with your name. How does it make you feel when you know that God's love for you is so deep that He gave His only Son for you?

3. Read John 13:34-35. Our love for God is authenticated by how we love others. If God is commanding something so very difficult, we know He will empower us to obey. Why not try praying for your husband? Perhaps begin by asking that God's love would lead him to repentance.

Chapter 3

Drop the Backpack, Dora!

"Be still and know that I am God..."

Psalm 46:10a

In the days after finding out about my husband's nearly decade-long infidelity, my mind felt chaotic. Panicked. Restless. I couldn't focus. I texted my sister, "I still can't sleep. I'm hungry. I'm not hungry. I'm tired. I'm not tired. I'm a mess." I was irritable with everyone around me.

The voice of the Enemy was loud and his lies were endless:

You're unloved.

You should have seen this coming.

You look like a fool.

You'll never make it on your own.

You're such a disgrace to your husband.

You're ugly.

You must have done something to cause this.

Sometimes, the painful thoughts announced themselves with the force of a Category 5 hurricane. To combat these attacks, I'd try to read my Bible study notes, but thoughts and images would start to fast-forward through my mind, causing me turmoil. Other times, the thoughts would creep in slowly. I would lay awake at night, tears streaming down my face, as I recounted memories in which I thought we'd been happy.

I pictured Will last year, after hours of digging and planting, dirt on his clothes, showing me the dream garden he had built for our family. I saw us during the COVID quarantine deciding to buy chickens, him building the Pinterest-style henhouse I had picked out for our baby chicks. I could see us years before that, exploring the entire Western US in our travel trailer, watching sunrises and sunsets together.

When I woke up, I would use any energy I had gained from my brief, restless sleep to piece together the timelines of his affairs. I was trying to make sense of years of lies and felt frustrated to be working through these new hurts and betrayals by myself. Will was physically there, sleeping soundly next to me, but emotionally, I was alone.

His conscience was clean for the first time in a decade. He knew he had a lot of work ahead of him, but his confession had brought him closer to the Truth than he had been in years. In John 14:6, Jesus claimed to be "the way and the truth and the life." Jesus, the Truth, calls us out of darkness and into His light, so sin is no longer our master (Romans 6:14).

I felt out of control; my mind WAS out of control. I'd never suffered from anxiety, but now my life was falling apart. I needed to gain a sense of control.

My first impulse was to go, find, do. I opened my own bank account. I called my boss and told her that for reasons I couldn't explain, I wouldn't be able to work for a few weeks. I made an appointment to be tested for STDs. I debated calling a divorce lawyer.

As the panic mounted, I even tried to step down from my leadership role at Bible study.

One morning, after the big kids had gone to school and my husband to work, I sat at the dining room table, staring at the family photos on the wall. We had three beautiful children with toothy smiles and matching shirts. We'd paid a reputable and expensive photographer to take us to a picturesque location for the shoot, then afterwards, bought matching picture frames for our favorite portraits. Now, every time I noticed them, disgust would lump up in the pit of my stomach. For four of us, it was the "before." Our smiles were genuine, our lives relatively pain-free. But for the fifth member of our family, Will, I now knew it was the "during," when lies, deception, and sin were welling up in his mind and his actions. I took every family photo down from the walls that day.

The world around me didn't stop. I had to act normal. My husband had just come home from deployment, and the kids hadn't seen him in eight months. I couldn't ruin their reunion by telling them what he'd done, and the boys had no clue what was happening. We ate dinner together, drove to church together, and rode our bikes together on the weekends, just like we did in the before times. The boys would chat incessantly about events at school or the newest books they had read, and Will and I would respond to them with warmth and excitement. The kids still needed our help with homework. Someone had to go grocery shopping, and the dishes kept piling up. Meanwhile, Will and I both silently wondered what the next step was going to be.

Thankfully, since the hallway walls were bare of photos, my gaze constantly turned to the only decoration that was left, a wooden sign with Exodus 14:14 printed on it. My sister had given it to me several years back, and it had become a favorite Bible verse:

"The LORD will fight for you;
you need only to be still."

Over the next few weeks, I discovered that there was, indeed, a spiritual battle to be fought - only I wasn't the one who was going to fight it. Ephesians 6:12 reminds us, "For our struggle is not against flesh and blood, but against the rulers, against the authorities, against the powers of this dark world and against the spiritual forces of evil in the heavenly realms." While my husband did choose his actions, there was a greater force at work. Ultimately, Will wasn't my enemy (though I felt like he was). The Lord was whispering to me, through His Word, that my only job was to be still.

"Be still" is written several times in the Bible. When the Israelites came to a halt at the Red Sea and the enemy was in hot pursuit, Moses confidently told the people, "The LORD will fight for you; you need only to be still" (Exodus 14:14). Immediately after this, the Lord miraculously parted the Red Sea, protected His children, and destroyed the enemy. We know God CAN; that's His nature. We also know, sometimes His answer is "No," or "Wait." Your marriage won't suddenly repair itself. Your husband might not come to you on his knees begging for forgiveness. Even if he does, recovery can be a long and difficult journey. Right now, God's asking you to be still in His presence and wait on Him.

I was watching *Dora and the Lost City of Gold*© with my kids last night. Dora and her friends got caught in quicksand, but Dora knew how to escape. She told them to stop panicking, lean back, and make slow movements. I wondered if this was good advice (just in case I ever find myself in Amazonian quicksand), so I Googled it and read the steps.

First, take off anything weighing you down. Next, stay calm and don't make frantic movements. The more you struggle, the harder it will be to escape. Don't walk forward; instead, take small steps to the side. If you're unable to free yourself, lean back and take deep breaths. Leaning back will spread your weight more evenly, and you'll be more buoyant with air in your lungs. From there, you can do a backstroke and wiggle your feet up to the surface. This is exactly what Dora and her friends had done, and it worked!

I went to bed last night comforted by two things. First, as long as my kids are watching Dora, I can have confidence in their ability to safely explore the banks of the Amazon River. Second, the directions for escaping real quicksand closely resemble the directions for escaping spiritual quicksand. Does it feel like you're caught in quicksand? Does every new detail of the betrayal cause you to sink deeper and deeper into what seems like unavoidable destruction?

In Psalm 46:10a, God encourages us by saying: "Be still, and know that I am God." What does remaining still look like? Being still involves actively waiting. It's releasing that heavy backpack of burdens to God, avoiding BIG steps, and waiting instead for God's answers. It's leaning back into His capable arms, taking a deep breath, and taking your time. It may seem like you have only two choices right now: leave or ask your husband to leave. Separation is a reasonable choice in many scenarios, but remember that nothing has to be decided immediately. Wait for God and listen for His guidance.

I need to emphasize that obedience does not mean remaining in a physically or emotionally abusive relationship. You are not a doormat or scapegoat for abuse. The safety of yourself and your children is your highest priority.

Psalm 37:7a commands us to "Be still before the LORD and wait patiently for Him." The same psalm includes several actions to take that delight the Lord. This psalm teaches us that being still is not inactivity, but that resting in Him is wise and righteous activity. We can walk in obedience when we answer the call found in this psalm.

Just before this command, the psalmist writes in verse 5, "Commit your way to the LORD." This might involve letting go of trying to control your husband's behavior and trusting God with the results. Later, in verse 26, we're told to give generously. This could include giving up a free weekend to serve at church, or continuing to tithe, even when your single income is tight. Verse 23 speaks of delighting in Him, something we can do by opening up God's Word and spending time with Him.

The more we know of God, the more easily we can put these commands into practice. It's not easy, especially when working on a broken relationship, but we can obey. Nothing needs to be decided right now. Nothing is a surprise to God. He knows what the future holds. Dig into His Word and commit your way to Him. He is your safety.

Wait on Him. Be still. Don't rush. See what God will do! Lean into the hands that made the universe, trusting that He will not let the quicksand swallow you.

Prayer for Today

Lord, when it feels like there's nothing more I can do to keep my head above the quicksand, remind me that I don't have to fight at all. You are with me. I choose to be still and wait on You. Quiet my heart and my mind as I look to Your Word for direction and guidance. As I bring my anxieties to You, please guard my heart and mind with Your peace that surpasses understanding.

Questions to Ponder

1. Why is remaining still so difficult? Sometimes it's not a physical stillness that you need, but a stillness in your soul. Consider dedicating a specific time and place to regularly practice stillness.

2. Read Luke 10:38-42. What do you learn about our Savior by His response to Martha? How would your life be different if you choose to sit quietly at the Lord's feet like Mary did?

3. In Mark 4:37-41, Jesus calmed a storm with His voice. What does this say about His power and His care for you? How does knowing this give you confidence?

Chapter 4

No Promise
He Won't Keep

"When you pass through the waters, I will be with you; and when you pass through the rivers, they will not sweep over you.

When you walk through the fire, you will not be burned; the flames will not set you ablaze."

Isaiah 43:2

I always knew Will as dependable, strong, and loyal. He was a person who always did the right thing, even when no one was looking. He treated me and our children well. He was the last man on earth I imagined would have an affair, but then he confessed.

I was shocked. Blindsided. Sixteen years of trust disintegrated to dust in that moment. The man I had trusted the most, the man I had promised my life to, was the man who had done the most harm to me.

I questioned my own judgment, too. Deception had been happening right under my nose for years, and I had never realized it. I'd been beguiled. I felt like a fool. Had I been denying red flags all along? Could I even trust my own intuition anymore?

Nothing felt certain. What else could he be lying about? This behavior wasn't consistent with the man I knew. It was an incredible waste of time, but felt so necessary to try to sort out the truth from the lies. He had confessed to everything and answered every difficult question, but I still felt like I needed more truth. I would stay up all night scrolling back through years and years of text messages, social media feeds, browsing histories, bank statements, and phone records. I was looking for more proof, but it never fixed anything. Actually, the more details I knew, the worse it hurt.

Will's betrayal affected my trust in other people, too. I began to question the integrity and motives of almost every man I encountered. I started labeling each man "guilty" until proven innocent. I avoided eye contact with men. Every time a man opened a door for me, I would cringe inside because I assumed that instead of being polite, he just wanted to see my backside. After I read the staggering statistics of how many Christian men regularly view pornography, I threw every coworker, pastor, waiter, clerk, and friend of Will's—basically the entire male species—into that category.

After Will confessed to me, I read this quote somewhere: "The Bible doesn't tell you to trust your husband. It tells you to trust God." I don't remember where I saw it, but I held onto it like a treasure. It was invaluable to me during our recovery. Later, I found Psalm 118:8: "It is better to take refuge in the LORD than to trust in humans," and Isaiah 2:22a: "Stop trusting in mere humans, who have but a breath in their nostrils." People can lie, cheat, steal, and disappoint. God was reminding me that only He is perfectly trustworthy. Even if my future seemed insecure, He would steadfastly be there with me.

God has NEVER been unfaithful, so trusting Him isn't risky behavior. Psalm 25:3 even tells us that the one who trusts in the Lord will never be put to shame. God doesn't need to earn our trust; He's got a great track record of being who He says He is and doing what He says He'll do. He's perfect.

Even knowing this, putting my trust in God wasn't always easy, and it occasionally wavered. Sometimes, to be less afraid, I would try to control the outcome of a situation. I told myself that I needed to ask the right questions, track my husband's every move, and not give him too much access to my heart. Some days, I leaned on my own understanding and tried to forge my own path through recovery. I read lots of books and articles about addictions and betrayal. I thought if I could understand why my husband cheated, I could prevent him from cheating on me in the future. I wasn't even sure we had a future. None of this helped my anxiousness. Our hearts are most content when we choose to surrender the situation to God and trust Him with the process.

During my recovery, I often clung to the Psalms. The Psalms repeatedly speak about the importance of trusting God, the blessings that come with that trust, and the reasons to trust Him. God is worthy. He doesn't make promises that He won't keep. God doesn't abandon us when circumstances are hard, and He never says or does anything unloving or unfair. He is good all the time and in every way. Check out these promises:

- ♥ "Some trust in chariots and some in horses, but we trust in the name of the LORD our God" (Psalm 20:7).

- ♥ "For the word of the LORD is right and true; he is faithful in all he does." (Psalm 33:4)

- ♥ "For great is your love, higher than the heavens; your faithfulness reaches to the skies." (Psalm 108:4)

- ♥ "The works of his hands are faithful and just; all his precepts are trustworthy." (Psalm 111:7)

- ♥ "All your commands are trustworthy." (Psalm 119:86a)

- ♥ "Let the morning bring me word of your unfailing love, for I have put my trust in you." (Psalm 143:8a)

- ♥ "The LORD is trustworthy in all He promises and faithful in all He does." (Psalm 145:13b)

In His goodness and grace God has given us many examples of His trustworthiness throughout Scripture. He did this for Peter, in

Matthew 14:27-33, inviting him to come to Him on the water. Peter eagerly stepped out of the boat and walked on the water towards Jesus. When Peter's faith wavered because of the wind, Jesus didn't let him drown, neither did He chastise him for being afraid. Instead, Jesus reached out His hand, caught Peter, and asked him, "Why did you doubt?" He was showing Peter, while defying the law of gravity, that He could be trusted.

Another test of faith is recounted in the story of Shadrach, Meshach, and Abednego in the fiery furnace. King Nebuchadnezzar commanded these men to worship the image of gold he had created. If they refused to bow, they would be thrown into a furnace. Their answer to the king? "King Nebuchadnezzar,.. If we are thrown into the blazing furnace, the God we serve is able to deliver us from it, and he will deliver us from Your Majesty's hand" (Daniel 3:16-17).

As King Nebuchadnezzar promised, the three men were bound and thrown into the fire. (He was so mad at them he heated the furnace to seven times hotter than usual). As God promised, He didn't leave His children alone. Three men were thrown in the furnace, but when King Nebuchadnezzar peered inside, he saw four men. Not only were they alive, but they also were unbound, unharmed, and walking around the furnace. God didn't abandon them, He entered into the suffering with them. When King Nebuchadnezzar saw this miracle, he acknowledged the God of Shadrach, Meshach, and Abednego saying, "They trusted in him and defied the king's command and were willing to give up their lives rather than serve or worship any god except their own God" (Daniel 3:28).

Does it feel like you're drowning in worry or anxiety? Are you wondering how you'll put dinner on the table without your husband's paycheck or retirement pension? What will you say when your toddler demands that Daddy tuck him in? Maybe the waves of doubt are so steady that you think you'll always feel worthless and unloved. Maybe you feel like you're actually suffocating, unable to grab that fresh breath of peace in between the sobs of hopelessness.

Perhaps the furnace has been turned up to seven times hotter than usual: your husband's pornography addiction has led him to physical infidelity or maybe he's cheated before, only this time he doesn't want to return home. It's possible that this was the last time, and now you're facing divorce. Maybe your children have been affected. Are you finding yourself trapped in a vortex of flames so hot that you'd rather die than feel their burn?

Whether you're feeling the impending crush of the waves or heat of the fire, there is someone in the midst of the sea and by your side in the blaze. The One who offers you hope is your trustworthy Jesus. He's telling you not to fear because He is here. God told the prophet Isaiah the same thing:

Do not fear, for I have redeemed you;
I have summoned you by name; you are mine.
When you pass through the waters,
I will be with you;
and when you pass through the rivers,
they will not sweep over you.
When you walk through the fire,
you will not be burned;
the flames will not set you ablaze.
For I am the LORD your God,
the Holy One of Israel, your Savior. (Isaiah 43:1-3)

Every storm and every fire in life serves as an opportunity to seek and know the Lord. It's hard to trust someone if you don't know his or her character. As you spend time reading the Bible, you will get to know God's attributes better. Once you understand the truth of His character, and begin to look for the expressions of it in your day-to-day life, you will learn you can trust Him to write your story. This takes time and intentionality. I encourage you to keep track of the ways that the Lord proves that He means what He says. It's helpful to have your own evidence as a reference.

Putting your trust in Jesus is not naiveté or passivity, and it's never a risk. Even if you never understand the purpose in this suffering, you can trust the process of healing from betrayal, taking comfort in His capable hands. God knows this is challenging when you're still reeling from the destruction of trust in your marriage. He will reach out His hand to you as He did for Peter. He will enter into the fire with you, as He did for Shadrach, Meshach, and Abednego. Through kindness and grace, with patience, He will prove trustworthy to every doubting heart.

Prayer for Today

Lord, I might not trust my husband right now, but I choose to trust You. Every word You speak is trustworthy. Please help me conquer my fear of the unknown. I have faith in the promise that You will never leave me.

Questions to Ponder

1. Since discovering betrayal in your marriage, how have you been reconsidering God's trustworthiness? Read Isaiah 43:2-3. How does this passage make you feel about placing your trust in God?

2. How have you witnessed Jesus "enter into the fire" with you? Write down each time you remember Him supporting you. Read what you've written the next time you start having feelings of doubt.

3. When you read the Bible, look for God's promises. Start with Romans 10:9-11. How can trusting in God's promises help you persevere?

Chapter 5

Beauty from Ashes

"To bestow on them a crown of beauty instead of ashes,
the oil of joy instead of mourning, and a garment of praise instead of a
spirit of despair."

Isaiah 61:3b

His office smelled like dude. Not a bad smell, just not very inviting for a woman. I was cautious. I knew his wife from Bible study, and I was horrified that she might find out the dirty secret. Surely, it wasn't the first time he had witnessed a marriage devastated by years of lies and infidelity. Still, shame and embarrassment overwhelmed me. *Everyone who had just watched us walk in must know. They all must think I'm a fool. How could I have not known?* I sat next to the trash can, thinking I might throw up.

Yesterday, the rest of the truth came out, and my heart hadn't stopped pounding since. I was sick, and so angry. It felt wrong to be in the pastor's office when my insides felt so disgusting. I felt ashamed of my husband. He needed to suffer. I wished horrible things on him. I wished horrible things on the other women.

Last night, when he told me, I responded, "I hate you." I thought if I could string the right words together at how utterly disgusted and repulsed I was by him, my stomach would feel better. I didn't want to be in the same room as him, let alone sitting in a chair next to him.

I didn't know what our pastor might say. I secretly hoped he would help me pour the guilt on thick, but maybe not. I didn't want Will to get up and walk away too quickly. Maybe a slow trickle of shame would be better.

Yeah, right. Who was I kidding? There were probably some good ol' Christian clichés waiting for us. Our pastor would probably try to bypass the emotions and the trauma of it all and suggest we start some intense Bible work. He'd supply us with a list of local marriage counselors, and we'd walk out of the office with no hope.

The three of us sat in silence. Finally, the pastor broke it, stating, "This marriage is dead."

My thoughts halted. I held my breath. Hearing it out loud made it all too real.

I glanced over at Will who was staring blankly somewhere beyond our pastor's head. He didn't even flinch at the statement. Since he wouldn't make eye contact with me, I figured he agreed.

I had known for a long time that something was off in our marriage, but dead? When did it die? Just three days earlier I had shaved my legs, put on lipstick, and happily welcomed my husband home from an eight-month deployment.

The pastor continued: "The only way forward is to let God build a new marriage - from the ground up."

I exhaled and started to cry. I felt relieved, but at the same time, I didn't believe it could actually happen. Will was already checked out.

In Genesis chapter 18, Sarah eavesdrops on Abraham's conversation with God. She hears the Lord say: "I will surely return to you about this time next year, and Sarah your wife will have a son" (verse 10, ESV). I imagine her lifting her apron toward her mouth, trying to contain her laughter because this would have sounded ridiculous to her. She was way past the age to conceive, and Abraham was no spring chicken either!

The New Living Translation (NLT) actually quotes Sarah as asking herself, "How could a worn-out woman like me enjoy such pleasure, especially when my master—my husband—is also so old?" (verse 12).

Romans 4:19 gives some extra context about Abraham and Sarah's situation, describing Abraham's body as "as good as dead" and Sarah's womb as "dead" (verse 19).

The apron couldn't help Sarah hide from God. He addressed her faithlessness for what it was. "Why did Sarah laugh? Is anything too hard for the Lord?" (Genesis 18:13-14a, NLT).

Is rebuilding a marriage too hard for the Lord? The answer is no. God brought life to Sarah's dead womb. God never changes, and the way He dealt with people then is the same way He deals with people now. We can be assured that He is still able to bring restoration to broken and dead things. He restored a man's voice by driving the demons out of him (Matthew 12:22), made clean a man with leprosy (Mark 1:42), brought healing and health to a man's shriveled hand (Mark 3:5), made a deaf man hear by putting His fingers into his ears (Mark 7:33-35), and gave sight to a man by spitting on his eyes (Mark 8:23).

These are just a few of the miracles listed in the New Testament! The miracle-working God from the Bible is the same mighty God we serve today. There's no limit to what God can do with His endless resources and absolute power. We can be assured that our suffering is never wasted when placed in the hands of the Miracle Worker.

If your husband and you decide to forgive each other (as you too will also need grace in this process), and he turns away from his destructive patterns, then your marriage can be rebuilt. God is here. You can have hope and allow His grace to flow through you, enabling you to give it to your husband. Your marriage can be a beautiful picture of God's redemptive power. You can forgive because you have the power of the Holy Spirit in you and the example set by Jesus in His

Word. Choosing to rebuild a marriage, with God at the center, will take a lot of hard work from both of you, but it's certainly possible!

Rebuilding our marriage took constant prayer, months of marriage counseling, and each of us going to weekly recovery groups. We enrolled in a sixteen-week marriage class. We asked for help, prayer, and wise counsel from trusted friends and family. We spent time in God's Word together and listened to helpful Christian podcasts on the subject of betrayal. We showed patience and grace after being exposed to raw (and sometimes very ugly) emotions from the other person. We asked the Lord to give us His eyes to see each other. Our rebuilding even included leaving one job for another and moving the family to a new state! Later, we shared God's glory with others by inviting our closest family and friends to celebrate our 17th wedding anniversary with a vow renewal on the beach.

We are still "adding on" to the rebuild daily. We've found a new home church and Bible studies. In the mornings, we drink our coffee together with a devotional and prayer. We practice good communication habits and talk about concerns before they become issues. We have regular date nights. For certain triggers, we discuss plans of action. We initiate weekly check-ins, and all screen time and passwords are easily accessible to the other person. There can't be any secrets. Our marriage and home are secure, because this time they're built on the solid Rock of Jesus Christ (Matthew 7:24-27).

Your marriage may not be heading towards reconciliation and a vow renewal, but that doesn't mean that God isn't working to make beauty from its ashes. Maybe your husband has moved out or you've been divorced for some time already. Even if your life looks way different than you expected it to when you shared your wedding vows, God can still renew you. That's His business—bringing life from death.

Open up your Bible to Matthew 9:18-25. Read how Jairus, full of faith, asked Jesus to bring his daughter back to life. Jesus entered the room where she lay dead and said, "The girl is not dead but asleep" (verse 24). Jesus took her by the hand, and she got up.

In Luke chapter 7 we see another story of Jesus' life-resurrecting power. As Jesus and His disciples approached Nain, a town a few miles south of Nazareth, He saw that someone was being carried out of the gate on a bier, a type of open coffin used in that day. The young man, now dead, was the only person his mother had in life. She was a widow, and now, her only son was gone. He had probably been taking care of her and would have been her main source of financial security. Verse 12 displays Jesus' tenderness and compassion so beautifully: "When the Lord saw her, his heart went out to her and he said, 'Don't cry.'"

He saw into this mother's pain. He saw the tears that were falling, and He had compassion on her. Jesus went to the man and said, "Young man, I say to you, get up!" (verse 14). The young man's life was restored, and he sat up and began to talk. The bystanders, amazed, praised God and shared the news with others. Verse 17 says that "This news about Jesus spread throughout Judea and the surrounding country." This life-giving miracle was all for His glory!

In John chapter 11, Jesus' beloved friend, Lazarus, walks out from his grave alive! Before Lazarus died, Jesus said in verse 4, "This sickness will not end in death. No, it is for God's glory so that God's Son may be glorified through it." Speaking to Jesus, one of Lazurus' sisters boldly proclaimed, "Lord, if you had been here, my brother would not have died" (verse 32). She couldn't yet see the beauty that would come from bearing witness to Lazarus' resurrection.

Similarly, Jairus, when he traveled to meet Jesus, certainly wasn't thinking his life was going according to plan. As he left his dead daughter at home to seek out Jesus, it didn't feel like there would ever be a time when he'd be tucking her into bed again or sending her off to collect the day's water. God took Jairus' tears and wove them into a beautiful story of borrowed time.

Before meeting Jesus, perhaps that widow whose only son had died thought to herself, "It's not supposed to be this way. A mother shouldn't outlive her son." At that time, she wasn't able to see the end of the story when she'd hold him in her arms again.

Sarah didn't understand either. How many nights did she grieve the loss of the life she thought she'd have, as another birthday placed her a year further away from childbearing age? She didn't think it would be that way, but she couldn't see ahead to the promised child God would give her in her old age.

We are the same way, aren't we? Sometimes, I can't see the end clearly. I can't picture how my horrible situation could ever end up resolved. I begin to doubt that things will ever be okay, but God, in His kindness and wisdom, has the power to make things more than okay. In Isaiah, He promised:

To console those who mourn in Zion,
To give them beauty for ashes,
The oil of joy for mourning,
The garment of praise for the spirit of heaviness;
That they may be called trees of righteousness,
The planting of the Lord, that He may be glorified. (Isaiah 61:3, NKJV)

God's way of making beauty doesn't always come in ways we'd expect. I'd be remiss if I didn't mention here the most powerful display of God's resurrection power ever known to man. Jesus Christ, the Perfect Lamb of God, was sacrificed on behalf of each of us. Every sin that you and I have ever committed and will ever commit, was placed on Jesus. He took the punishment and surrendered His life on the cross of Calvary so we would no longer stand guilty before God. He died a sinner's death, spent three days in a sealed grave, and miraculously rose to life again.

Jesus says to John in a vision, recorded in Revelation 1:18, "I am the Living One; I was dead, and now look, I am alive forever and ever!" What a feat! Jesus' death and resurrection is the most creative, selfless, mind-boggling, merciful answer to the death that sin causes. Something no one but God could put together!

Peter, who Jesus described as, "The rock I will build my church on" (Matthew 16:18), gave the following sermon about this in the book of Acts chapter 2:

Fellow Israelites, listen to this: Jesus of Nazareth was a man accredited by God to you by miracles, wonders and signs, which God did among you through him, as you yourselves know. This man was handed over to you by God's deliberate plan and foreknowledge; and you, with the help of wicked men, put him to death by nailing him to the cross. But God raised him from the dead, freeing him from the agony of death, because it was impossible for death to keep its hold on him. (verses 22-24)

Jesus' story did not end in death. There is victory! Jesus is still alive, seated at the right hand of God the Father. The ugliness of our sin was erased. We now have the opportunity to have a relationship with God. We are alive, forgiven, and free because of Jesus' death and resurrection. That's the most beautiful death-to-life story ever told.

Perhaps the beauty isn't going to come from a restored marriage, but from God being glorified through your restored soul and beautifully healed heart. Just the other evening, when I attended a women's event at my church, we were asked to write notes of godly encouragement to women who work at strip clubs. By being able to write a note without bitterness spoiling my words, I see how the Lord has healed the anger in my heart. Recently at work, I took care of a pregnant woman who had conceived a baby in adultery. By having compassion on this woman, I see another manifestation of how the Lord has healed the anger in my heart. When I can tell my story of God's redemption without tears streaming down my face, I know God's done a miraculous work. During this season of intense pressure and darkness, as you've had the opportunity to know God better and trust Him more, your heart has probably been made to look more like His. I pray it has.

Do you know what else is made in the presence of intense pressure, extreme heat, and darkness? Diamonds. Billions of years ago, diamonds were formed deep within the earth with pressure exceeding

725,000 pounds per square inch. To put this in context, this pressure is nearly 200 times more than that of a crocodile's bite! Deep below ground, this pressure, combined with temperatures of 2,100 degrees Fahrenheit, transformed carbon atoms into the most precious and beautiful gems in the world. When you're feeling the heat and pressure from every side, there's potential for beauty. Your heart shines like a gorgeous, glistening diamond when you choose to depend on Christ for everything you need and release your fears to Him. It shines when you worship and praise Him, and follow Him in faith and obedience. Remember, diamonds shine brightest against a dark background. In all of this, the glory of God is on display!

I pray that regardless of how your story turns out, you find yourself singing like David in Psalm 30:11-12: "You turned my wailing into dancing; you removed my sackcloth and clothed me with joy, that my heart may sing your praises and not be silent. LORD my God, I will praise you forever." I'm asking God to bestow on you a crown of beauty instead of ashes, the oil of joy instead of mourning, and a garment of praise instead of a spirit of despair. May you be like an oak of righteousness – a display of His splendor (Isaiah 61:3).

Prayer for Today

Lord, I've known You as Miracle Worker. I've seen You make a way where there is no way by transforming impossible situations into stories of healing and new life. I pray that You would take the devastation brought by this betrayal and resurrect something beautiful in me. It's all for Your glory!

Questions to Ponder

1. In what ways have you witnessed the Lord transform beauty and new life into your story?

2. How does the ending of the story in Luke 7:11-17 encourage you to share with others what God has done in your life?

3. Healing from the trauma of betrayal isn't a quick or easy process. What favorite verses can you cling to, even if you can't yet see past the devastation?

Chapter 6

Jesus Wept, Too

"Praise be to the God and Father of our Lord Jesus Christ, the Father of compassion and the God of all comfort, who comforts us in all our troubles, so that we can comfort those in any trouble with the comfort we ourselves receive from God."

2 Corinthians 1:3-4

I texted my sisters and my mom: "Is it weird that I'm kind of excited for my first night at my betrayal support group?" It had only been ten days since D-Day, but the Lord had been at work for months arranging the details of this very night. It's bittersweet to think that He had foreseen the circumstances of each woman who would come to our group, and the agony in which they would find themselves. He was saddened by the sins of their husbands long before these women would discover the heartbreaking news. He had comforted the leaders of the group in their own troubles so that they could now comfort us in ours (2 Corinthians 1:4).

When I walked into the church meeting room that night, I was dumbfounded. *Why were the leaders smiling? What was there to be happy about?* I noticed that even though it was evening, their makeup was still intact. Why wasn't their mascara smeared under their eyes like mine? How could a person whose heart had been broken still manage to make the effort to wear lipstick? One gal was arranging the desserts, pastries and sweets on the counter. How could anyone here feel like eating? At the same, it didn't look like enough food to solve my problems. I wanted to stuff both my face and my feelings.

"Hey, Robin, welcome!" a voice called out from behind me. I turned around to see Jessie, the group leader who had called me when I signed up a few days ago. She smiled and hugged me. It was our first time meeting in person, but I immediately felt comforted by her embrace. By virtue of the nature of the group, her presence meant she had also suffered great loss and betrayal, but here she was, overflowing with love from the God of comfort Himself.

As women began to trickle in, I saw beauty in the room: young and middle-aged women, women of different skin tones, women of all body shapes. One woman wore a pregnancy glow and the most adorable maternity overalls.

The meeting started and the women talked. They spoke words of empathy, kindness, and wisdom. I watched as body postures started to relax and nervous expressions turned to joy-filled smiles. I felt compassion for each woman and appreciated their non-judgmental understanding of me and my situation. We'd all walked a bit in each other's scuffed-up shoes. After just an hour with them, I found my countenance had changed, too. For the first time in ten days, my soul was truly at peace. I was in the presence of the King's daughters. He was working through them to comfort me.

I had expected attending this support group would be the worst kind of awkward. Instead, it became my place of refuge, a space where I found the most comfort during the week. I didn't have to hide. These women understood what I was going through all too well.

We encouraged each other by sharing small victories each week. Soon, I shared one of my own via text in the group chat: "Don't stop praying. You will get to see miracles. One miracle so far... I haven't cried in two days." Our group always acknowledged these small victories and praised God for His hand in them. Other weeks we mourned the continual cycle of sin that some husbands were choosing. We replaced the Enemy's lies with the truth of God's Word. We helped each other see ourselves the way God saw us.

This group allowed me to see the comfort in action that Paul speaks about in 2 Corinthians 1:3-4, "Praise be to the God and Father of our Lord Jesus Christ, the Father of compassion and the God of all comfort, who comforts us in all our troubles, so that we can comfort those in any trouble with the comfort we ourselves receive from God."

Each of these women had walked – or was walking – where I had walked. Our stories looked different, but they had all experienced the soul-crushing misery that came with the realization of being betrayed. We shared similar fears and experienced similar losses. Most importantly, each of us had turned to God for comfort, and after we were comforted, were willing to let that comfort flow out towards others. I found new meaning in Proverbs 11:25, which says, "Whoever refreshes others will be refreshed." My problems weren't resolved, nor was my marriage fixed, but God, through His daughters, was refreshing me in my worst time of hurt.

Maybe you're looking for a safe place to run for refuge and solidarity. I hope you can experience the sense of community and comfort that I felt by having a group of people say, "I've been there, too." This problem is too difficult and maybe too complicated to go it alone.

It might not be safe or wise to share your struggles with certain friends or family members, especially if they tend to offer unsolicited opinions or unbiblical advice. Sometimes well-intentioned advice, coming from the wrong source, can hinder your recovery or cause additional, unnecessary grief. We need and want the support, but we don't need to seek it from people who aren't trustworthy. People who don't understand the gravity of the situation or who respond ignorantly to your sharing of your situation should be grouped into this category.

When dealing with the sensitive topic of your husband's sexual sin, it's wise to have a small group of Christian women who have already navigated the betrayal of their partners. Confide in them. Pray with them. Learn from them. Receiving support and guidance from fellow disciples of Jesus can help you fix your eyes on Him, and honor Him in your thoughts, words, and actions. Working towards personal healing (and possibly marital healing) is possible with the support of God and community.

Our Lord was also betrayed. Not only did Judas betray Jesus for a mere thirty pieces of silver, but he did it also with a conniving, deceitful kiss. "Now the betrayer had arranged a signal with them: 'The one I kiss is the man; arrest him.' Going at once to Jesus, Judas said, 'Greetings, Rabbi!' and kissed him" (Matthew 26:48-49). If Judas is named "the betrayer," that means that Jesus was the One who was betrayed. Who better to empathize with us than someone who has experienced the same hurt?

Jesus knows exactly what it feels like to be disregarded, disowned, and abandoned by those who said they'd stick with you to the end. While eating the Last Supper with Jesus, Peter told Him, "'Even if all fall away on account of you, I never will... Even if I have to die with you, I will never disown you.' And all the other disciples said the same" (Matthew 26:33-35). That very evening, after Jesus was arrested by men with swords and clubs, every single disciple—his best friends and closest followers—deserted Him.

We're not told where the other disciples went, but Peter quietly followed after Jesus to the courtyard of the high priest, just outside of where Jesus was being tried. He wanted to see what would happen. This was Peter's Lord. He had been the first disciple to declare to Jesus, "You are the Messiah, the Son of the living God" (Matthew 16:16).

Was he horrified by the hostility towards his best friend? Perhaps he heard the crowd taunting Jesus, spitting in His face and shouting, "Prophesy!" Was he breathless every time his Lord had the wind knocked out of him? It didn't matter what Peter's feelings or emotions were, because in the end he chose denial. Three times Peter was presented with the option of sticking with Jesus or denying him and three times he chose betrayal.

There's a tiny detail, only in the Gospel of Luke: "The Lord turned and looked straight at Peter" (Luke 22:61a).

What a heartbreaking image.

Jesus experienced a moment of truth that shattered His life, too. The eyes of the betrayer met the eyes of the betrayed. Because Jesus' own heart has broken from the pain of betrayal from Judas and Peter, He knows how to comfort you. He's been there. He understands.

One of the most tender moments in the Bible is in John 11:35: "Jesus wept." Jesus didn't hide His grief.

Lazarus, a friend whom Jesus loved, had just died. His sisters Mary and Martha were confused about why Jesus had taken so long to come to them. They had sent word to Jesus that Lazarus was sick, but Jesus took His time in getting to them. Lazarus died before Jesus arrived, and both sisters said to Jesus, "If you had been here, my brother would not have died" (John 11:21, 32). When Jesus saw Mary grieving, the Bible says that He was deeply moved in spirit. He wept.

In the original language of this story, Koine Greek, the type of crying Jesus does is described differently from the type of crying the crowd gathered at Lazarus' tomb was doing. In John 11:35, *dakryō* is used to describe Jesus' crying, meaning He was shedding quiet tears of grief. The word chosen to describe the crying of the crowd in John 11:33 was *klaiō*, meaning they were wailing. It was customary in that time to display one's grief outwardly, especially when associated with death. People might wail, tear their clothing, and even hire professional mourners. Jesus' tears weren't just following tradition or custom. They were a personal expression of grief. His tears portrayed empathy and concern for the friends who had just lost their brother. Jesus understands our pain and grieves with us. He wants to comfort us.

God is close to the brokenhearted and saves those who are crushed in spirit (Psalm 34:18). Allow Him, the God of comfort, to wipe the tears from your eyes and dry your face. He's the God of unlimited resources and there is no limit to how He might provide comfort. I pray that, like me, you can find a safe group of women who will welcome you with dessert, pray with you, and support you through this process. When you find them, let them help. Let that comfort flow from you to shepherd those who also need it. Chances are, He's already arranging the details.

Prayer for Today

Lord, when I feel like no one else can understand the hurt I'm processing, remind me of the ways You've been hurt, too. Comfort me with the comfort that can only come from You so that I can—in turn and in time—comfort others who are in need.

Questions to Ponder

1. What does the verse, "Jesus wept" (John 11:35) show you about God's character? In what ways has He comforted you recently? How can you show Him gratitude?

2. Read Isaiah 53:3. How does understanding this truth help you when you feel like God is distant or unfamiliar with your pain?

3. Second Corinthians 1:4 encourages us to comfort those in trouble with the comfort we ourselves receive from God. What woman in your life could use some comfort from you today? How can you show genuine compassion to her?

Chapter 7

Alaska:
The Hopeful Frontier

"We have this hope as an anchor
for the soul, firm and secure."

Hebrews 6:19a

Less than three weeks had passed since my husband's disclosure, and the two of us were on a flight to spend an entire week in Alaska. We wrestled with the thought of not going on the all-expenses-paid trip, but we had been selected for it months ago by a Christian non-profit organization. We had already booked the flights, lined up childcare, and asked for time off work. We figured that even if we didn't talk the entire time, we would still benefit from the much-needed distraction from the hell we were walking through.

The goal of the program was to bring rest and rejuvenation to wounded military veterans and their spouses through marriage enrichment. I had read several articles about attendees' life-changing experiences. Couples had surrendered their lives and marriages to Jesus, gotten baptized, and even renewed their wedding vows (Imagine!) as a result of the program. God had known that our marriage would be in shambles at the very time we were scheduled for the trip, right when we would need it most.

Satan would have loved nothing more than to see us cancel our trip. The day before leaving, it was obvious that he was hard at work to prevent us from going. Our oldest son suddenly came down with a severe cough, and in the first year of COVID, this was a huge opportunity for panic. We hurried to the ER to get him tested for COVID. We found out the cough was a reaction to a food allergy. Crisis averted.

Later that night, our middle son started throwing up. Again, we worried about leaving sick children in the care of their grandparents, but my in-laws insisted that we carry on with the plans. Despite the enemy's scheming, we flew out early the next morning. "Of course, because God is in control," ended up becoming our family motto soon after our return home.

On our trip over, I daydreamed about the miracles I hoped for in our marriage. Will is an avid outdoorsman who feels safest, happiest, and most at peace when he's in nature. I sensed that God was going to use the beautiful scenery of Alaska to draw Will close to his Creator. There was so much repair that needed to happen in our relationship.

This trip, free from the demands of work and children, was the perfect opportunity to begin healing. We would have access to spiritual counsel all week long—surely Will would take the opportunity to talk to one of the chaplains. I prayed he would surrender his guilt and accept the forgiveness being offered. We'd hopefully get on track towards healing and recovery. Maybe Will would even have the desire to renew our wedding vows. Actually, surely he would! With the backdrop of a glassy lake, poplar and fir trees, and snowcapped mountains, there was no better place.

Despite what we had been experiencing prior to arrival, once there, it felt like Heaven on earth. On the first night, we sat down for dinner with the other couples at a table that looked like it could hold the entire wedding feast of Heaven. The servers addressed us by name, even though they had never met us, because all the staff had been praying for us for weeks before we arrived. I imagine being greeted similarly through Heaven's gates! Our brothers and sisters in Christ treated us like distinguished guests and made us feel like royalty. Even the cleaning staff prayed for us as they made our beds and emptied our trash cans every day. They let us know by leaving little handwritten notes with words of encouragement on our nightstand.

Will and I loved the sights and sounds of Alaska: the brown bears catching and tearing apart salmon with their giant canines, rainbows stretching across the lake, and float planes whirring to a landing on water runways. We went fly fishing in the rain. We walked under a 35-foot waterfall. We felt the thrill of wild turbulence on our private float plane tours. We ate well. Everything about the trip was perfect, but when we boarded the flight home, I felt overwhelmed with disappointment.

I didn't want to go home. I didn't think we were ready. Why hadn't God moved like I had expected Him to? I had been so sure that this trip would be the first chapter of our new story. I had texted those closest to me and told them to be ready to witness a miracle: Will and I were going to leave our "baggage" in Alaska. Instead, as the plane accelerated down the dirt runway, I caught his eyes, full of emotional unrest. He still felt like a stranger to me. When we'd spoken on the trip, his words conveyed cycles of shame and guilt. There was no freedom from the bondage of sin in him. In just a few moments, we'd be in the air, and the perfect opportunity for a miracle would be behind us.

I put in my earplugs, trying to silence the excruciating disappointment. I stayed composed long enough to smile through my tiny porthole at the community of believers who were waving goodbye to us. As I turned away from them and the plane took off, I started crying. I felt defeated and hopeless. Soon, a pile of wadded-up tissues crowded my lap.

I had placed all of my hope in that Alaska experience, believing it would be the cure-all that would resurrect our dead marriage. I was more interested in witnessing my imaginary miracles than I was in trusting the perfect timing and sovereignty of the Miracle Worker

Himself. Much later in our recovery, I recognized the lifelong lesson that the Lord taught me that week: Placing my hope in anything or anyone other than Jesus leads only to disappointment and heartache.

The world defines "hope" much differently than the Bible. We use the word casually ("I hope you feel better soon," or, "We're hoping for a boy!"). It's simply desiring something to happen or be true. However, as Christians, it's important to understand that true hope isn't just wishful thinking. It's a confident assurance that what God promises in His Word will come to pass. Our hope comes from God's love and grace, His promise of salvation, and the fact that our eternal inheritance can never spoil or fade (1 Peter 1:4).

Before the beginning of time, God promised His children would have eternal life with Him (Titus 1:2). Isn't it beautiful that because He couldn't imagine the heartbreak of an eternity separated from His beloved children, He made a plan to make our relationship with Him right before we even existed? His love was too deep, too wide, and too big to leave us without hope (Ephesians 3:18). Because Jesus' death has atoned (paid) for our sins, God sees us as His holy daughters. Our sins have been forgiven, washed away with the blood of Jesus. Our filthy rags of sin have been exchanged for white robes of righteousness.

God invites us into a relationship which extends beyond the limits of time and space. It's a relationship that will never perish because no one can snatch us out of God's hand (John 10:29). At the moment of salvation, God even gives us His Holy Spirit as a guarantee of the glorious inheritance waiting for us! Our relationship with Him is living hope. This hope holds us steady when the storms of infidelity, betrayal, and addictions rage against us, attempting to crush our confidence in God's goodness. Our souls, nourished by this living hope, know the truth of who God is.

Jeremiah 23:16 warns us about putting our hopes in false prophets: "Do not listen to what the prophets are prophesying to you; they fill you with false hopes. They speak visions from their own minds, not from the mouth of the LORD." We might not have false prophets speaking in our ears, but there are many things that could fill us with false hopes. Treatment plans, tracking apps, social media groups, counseling programs, and accountability partners are all tools that the Lord might provide for you or your husband during your season of healing. Pray that God would give you the discernment to determine which tools are best for you.

The mistake happens when we attach our hope for healing to the tools instead of the One who does the healing. If your tools fail to perform miracles, you could end up just like me on that plane, crying out of despair with a mountain of crumpled tissues in your lap.

The author of Psalm 42:5 was also in a puddle of tears. He wrote about how his tears had been his food day and night. He said, "Why, my soul, are you downcast? Why so disturbed within me?" He knew that God was his only hope in his present circumstance. He turned his downcast countenance toward the God of hope, and read what he said: "Put your hope in God, for I will yet praise him, my Savior and my God." His disturbed soul was reminded of his hope in God and he began singing a song of praise.

God loves you too much to leave you without hope. He's not abandoning you in this flood of calamity. You're like a ship, tethered safely to Him. "For the LORD, the LORD himself is [your] Rock eternal" (Isaiah 26:4b). You can stand securely on the promises of God; remember how He's been faithful to you in the past. Your faith and hope will remain secure when you're anchored to the God of hope.

In mercy, Jesus Christ suffered on the cross so that the scarlet stains of your sins would be white as snow. He did it so you could be adopted as a child of God. Suffering is only temporary for those of us who have trusted in Jesus for salvation. One day, you'll be seated at the banquet table of Heaven where everything is made new. There will be no more death or mourning or crying or pain (Revelation 21:4b-c). You'll be in perfect relationship with the Lord forever and ever. Now that's a hope to burst into a song of praise about!

I share Paul's heart as he prays for his friends in Ephesians 1:18-19a: "I pray that the eyes of your heart may be enlightened in order that you may know the hope to which he has called you, the riches of his glorious inheritance in his holy people, and his incomparably great power for us who believe."

Prayer for Today

Lord, give my mind the strength to hold unswervingly to the hope I profess. I know that You promised me an eternal relationship with You, and You are forever faithful to Your Word. Let my tears be turned to praise, as I'm reminded that You are my only source of true hope.

Questions to Ponder

1. How does Psalm 42 give you confidence that it's okay to bring your lament to God?

2. While walking through this season of healing, in what practical ways can you guard your heart and mind from misplaced hope or unrealistic expectations?

3. Placing our hope securely in Jesus doesn't mean that we will have a life of simplicity and ease. Read Lamentations 3:19-25. How do these words help you reorient towards God, even in this trial?

Chapter 8

An Encounter
with El-Roi

"She gave this name to the Lord *who spoke to her:*
'You are the God who sees me,' for she said, 'I have now
seen the One who sees me.'"

Genesis 16:13

I remember Sunday school lessons from my childhood. Noah, in faith, built an ark which saved all of the animals and his family from the flood. Samuel learned how to discern God's voice when he was just a child. We studied the great heroes of the faith: Abel, Enoch, Noah, Abraham, Isaac, Jacob, Joseph, Moses, Joshua, Rahab, and many others who trusted in God.

I remember studying the not-so perfect moments: Eve falling into temptation, Jonah boarding a boat in disobedience, and Peter taking his eyes off Jesus while walking on water. My Sunday school teacher told us the story of how God visited Abraham and how Sarah had laughed when He said she would have a baby in her old age.

My teacher didn't spend much time on what Sarah and Abraham were doing prior to that story, though. You can read about it in Genesis 16, but here's the gist: As Sarah (who back then was called "Sarai") grew older, she didn't think she'd be able to conceive a child. Not trusting in God's timing, she decided to take matters into her own hands. She told her husband to sleep with her maidservant Hagar, in order for him to have an heir. Abraham (called 'Abram' then) impregnated Hagar, and she gave birth to Ishmael.

To put this in context, Hagar couldn't really give consent. She was a slave from another culture, being given as a "wife" to an eighty-six-year-old man, to act as a surrogate for Sarah. This practice was culturally acceptable, but I imagine Hagar felt used and abused. Once she was pregnant, Sarah mistreated her so badly that Hagar decided to run away. Rather than staying with the couple she knew would help her care for her child, she fled into the desert–pregnant, alone, and scared.

In this moment of rejection and despair, God saw Hagar. She stopped at a spring near the roadside, and suddenly, the angel of the LORD appeared. He called Hagar by name and acknowledged her misery, fears, and uncertainty (Genesis 16:7-12). He told her that not only would she have a son, Ishmael, but that her descendants would be too numerous to count.

God reassured Hagar but did not promise that her problems would go away. He sent Hagar right back to live with her biggest problem: the woman who had planned for her to get pregnant, then who became jealous and angry when her own plan worked! Her life didn't become easy, but God saw her and gave her new hope. She felt recognized, cared for. "She gave this name to the LORD who spoke to her: 'You are the God who sees me,' for she said, 'I have now seen the One who sees me'" (Genesis 16:13).

Was I seen like that? Did God notice me in my hurt? Was He watching as sin destroyed the things I thought to be true about my marriage? Did He notice the tears that soaked my pillow each night? Did He even care? Yes, yes, and YES! Psalm 121: 3-8 confirms it:

He will not let your foot slip—
he who watches over you will not slumber;
indeed, He who watches over Israel

will neither slumber nor sleep.
The LORD watches over you—
the LORD is your shade at your right hand;
the sun will not harm you by day,
nor the moon by night.
The LORD will keep you from all harm—
he will watch over your life;
the LORD will watch over your coming and going
both now and forevermore.

God hasn't turned His face away from you. The truth that seems nearly impossible to understand is that this situation isn't outside of God's knowledge. God sees everything, and we believe that He is also in control of every circumstance, so we can conclude that God has allowed it to happen. I wince even putting it in writing.

I don't have the answers as to why God has permitted this kind of destruction in your marriage. I do know that He is perfectly holy, meaning the betrayal you have experienced grieves Him. In Ezekiel 6:9, God shares His grief: "How I have been grieved by their adulterous hearts, which have turned away from me, and by their eyes, which have lusted after their idols." In the original language of this text, Hebrew, the word "grieved" means to break, to destroy, or to crush. In Ezekiel, God is communicating how broken-hearted He is that Israel has turned away from Him. The people have committed spiritual adultery by serving and lusting after worthless gods. God doesn't change. The God of the Old Testament Israelites is the same God whose heart is undoubtedly broken, destroyed, and crushed by the sins of lust, use of pornography, emotional affairs, and/or infidelity that have invaded your marriage. Remember, He designed marriage to represent the holy covenant that we have with Him.

As He empathizes with you and comforts your grieving heart, He will not allow your suffering to be wasted. In God's unexplainable economy, suffering can produce great results when we release control to Him. This may look like kneeling in your prayer closet, physically

61

opening your hands out to Him, and praying aloud, "Lord, it's all Yours. May Your will be done." It could also look like opening your Bible and asking God to reveal His heart to you as you read. God can initiate deeper spiritual growth in us when we are experiencing suffering. When we are most dependent on Him, His work is most noticeable. Paul, who suffered often, says in Romans 5:3-4 that suffering produces perseverance; perseverance, character; and character, hope. I can't explain God's ways, but I watched the process Paul wrote about happen in my life over the months that followed the disclosure.

Here's one of my journal entries after D-Day:

James 1:2-4 "Consider it pure joy, my brothers and sisters, whenever you face trials of many kinds, because you know that the testing of your faith produces perseverance. Let perseverance finish its work so that you may be mature and complete, not lacking anything."

I hate this verse. It sounds so nice when you hear a perfectly prepared sermon about it or read it as part of a women's Bible study, but when you are presently living through the worst pain imaginable, it's just stupid. Pure joy? You've got to be kidding me! Testing me? God, I've proven myself to you. You know that I live to honor You. I serve You. I'm teaching my children to know You. You already know my faith, and You have the power to make this pain stop. Yet, Your desire is to make me more like You. Lord, may You find that I continually honor You as my character grows.

God did equip me to do all things through His strength. I was able to persevere through the hard stuff: the gut-wrenching discovery questions in my support group, the forgiveness required to free my heart from bitterness, and the uncomfortable marriage counseling homework. My character was refined as my patience was tested, as I released the resentment harbored in my heart, and as my trust in the Lord grew deeper. I discovered true hope. It wasn't in the prospect of a healed marriage or a changed husband, but in the steadfast character of El Roi.

Because God is omnipresent (He has the ability to be everywhere at all times), He's seen you from the moment He formed you in your mother's womb. He watched you take your first hesitant and unsteady steps and later, barrel through your first white-knuckled drive. His eyes filled with delight the first time you recognized your need for Jesus. He celebrated with all of Heaven when you accepted His free gift of salvation. He lovingly gazed upon you as you prepared to exchange your wedding vows, and His gaze is still on you as you grieve your marriage that once was.

He has witnessed every single tear that has fallen from your eyes, and Psalm 56:8 says that He has each tear on record. Since He sees the past, the present, and the future, He can equip and prepare you to persevere in all you're called to do. When you allow God to have full reign in this process of faith testing and character growth, you'll be amazed at the work He will do in your heart! The hope that follows will not put you to shame, because God's love has been poured out into your heart through the Holy Spirit, who has been given to you (Romans 5:5).

Psalm 139:1-10 reassures us that God is aware of every circumstance and detail:

You have searched me, LORD,
and you know me.
You know when I sit down and when I rise;
you perceive my thoughts from afar.
You discern my going out and my lying down;
you are familiar with all of my ways.
Before a word is on my tongue
you, LORD, you know it completely.
You hem me in behind and before,
and you lay your hand upon me.
Such knowledge is too wonderful for me,
too lofty for me to attain.
Where can I go from your Spirit?

Where can I flee from your presence?
If I go up to the heavens, you are there;
if I make my bed in the depths, you are there.
If I rise on the wings of the dawn,
if I settle on the far side of the sea,
even there your hand will guide me,
your right hand will hold me fast.

The Angel of the LORD "found" Hagar at the spring, but God already knew where she was because He'd watched her flee into the desert. He knew she was pregnant because He already knew Ishmael's tiny heart fluttered inside her womb. Most important of all, He understood her tears because He had seen Sarah's treatment of her.

Our Father knows the road you're having to walk. His heart aches for the way you've been treated. He promises to be close to the brokenhearted and save those who are crushed in spirit (Psalm 34:18). May Hagar's story remind you that He will meet you in the desert. God sees you in your misery, fears, and uncertainty. He will be the collector of your tears, for He is El Roi, the God who sees.

Prayer for Today

Lord, I'm comforted by knowing that nothing is hidden from You. Thank You that I can't flee from Your view or Your presence. Open my eyes to see You, the One who sees me.

Questions to Ponder

1. Do you feel unseen, unheard, and abandoned? What does the way God responded to Hagar indicate about His character? What other Bible passages can you think of that show God searching for and/or seeking after His people?

2. How has God stepped into your situation to show you that He sees you?

3. Hagar praised God for being "the God who sees me." How might you respond to His loving compassion towards you?

Chapter 9

Look in the Mirror

"For you created my inmost being;
you knit me together in my mother's womb."

Psalm 139:13

Prior to D-Day, I had never struggled with feeling "less than." My body had changed as I'd gotten older, but so had the bodies of the women around me. We all had muffin tops, drooping eyelids, and acne scars. I wasn't bothered by these things, but my self-esteem shattered when I discovered I was no longer my husband's first choice.

I'd never had low self-esteem regarding my physical appearance. I'd also been bolstered by seeing the body positivity movement on social media: no-makeup challenges, posts of encouragement to "be authentic," and blogs about embracing who you are, stretch marks and all.

After Will told me that he wasn't physically attracted to me anymore, I loathed going to the gym. There were sexy women everywhere! They wore crop tops and spandex leggings. Some pushed double strollers around the track, looking like they should be models on the front of *Family Fun Magazine*©. They didn't need to wear makeup because their skin was so smooth. Everywhere I looked, they were there! I began comparing myself to them, constantly critiquing myself in their presence.

Have I let myself go? I wondered. I created stories about their perfect lives and had a running monologue in my head about them: *If my body looked like hers in that spandex, maybe he wouldn't have done it. Is it my teeth? Hers look so much whiter. How many crunches would I have to do to look good in that crop top? Her boobs are bigger, and she doesn't even have to wear glasses. I bet her husband never cheated on her.* In my mind, the lie became the truth: I was undesirable.

I need to stop right here.

I've discovered three things on this journey. First, the old breakup line from ninth grade actually applies: "It's not you, it's me." It's likely that your husband's struggle with lust was part of him before you started dating. It's not your weight or the size of your breasts or the smoothness of your skin. It's his sin nature.

Every human being is born into this world as a sinner (Psalm 51:5). We can choose to honor God with our thoughts, words, and deeds, or not. We are accountable for our choices. Sin is never forced upon us by someone else. We are told in 1 Corinthians 10:13 that God will never allow us to be tempted beyond what we can bear. He will always provide a way out of temptation. In regards to your husband's cheating, there's nothing you could have said or not said, nothing you could have done or not done, and no way that you could have looked or not looked, to prevent him from cheating. Infidelity is a choice, a decision. Despite God's promise to provide a way out of a tempting situation, your husband *chose* to give in to the desires of his flesh. Nothing about your appearance is to blame for his lust and infidelity. Sin is a condition of the heart. I'm so sorry if his choices made you think you were undesirable.

My second realization was about the sexy women at the gym: Every one of them is dealing with her own heartbreak, anxieties, and sin. They have also been created in God's own image, yet still struggle with their identities. Each one has her own discouraging thoughts about gray hairs, weight, or the shape of certain body parts. Compliment a woman who just got a new haircut, and you might hear it in her response: "Ugh. My hair is so thin. There's not much I can do with it," or "Thanks. I wish I could wear bangs like you do, though." Everything is not always as we perceive it.

My third (and favorite) realization was that I needed to see myself through God's eyes to see who I truly am. We are God's masterpiece creation. We were known and loved by Him before we were even born. In Psalm 139:13-14a, David says, "For you created my inmost being; you knit me together in my mother's womb. I praise you because I am fearfully and wonderfully made; your works are wonderful, I know that full well." This isn't just a quote for baby shower cards or nursery decorations. This is God's Word, which He allowed to be written hundreds of years ago so that we would know the truth today.

The Book of Job tells the story of a godly man who experiences unfathomable loss and pain. Despite his hardships, he recognizes the Lord as his Creator. The Bible says Job was blameless and upright; He feared God and shunned evil. He was considered the greatest man in his community (Job 1). He was successful in business, had a large family, and owned thousands of livestock. One day, Job lost everything. His oxen, donkeys, and camels were stolen, his servants were killed, his sheep burned to death, and his house collapsed, killing all of his children. Job was given no explanation for these heartbreaking tragedies. His friends shared their theories about why God had let this happen, but Job was careful to look to God first. He only sought God's answers.

Shortly after these tragedies, Satan afflicted Job with painful, miserable sores all over his body. The sores itched and oozed, making Job absolutely miserable. He began scraping himself with a piece of broken pottery, either to alleviate the unbearable itching or as a gesture of grief. He was in such anguish and was grieving so deeply that he wished he had never been born. (Can you relate?)

Job was angry and in pain. He voiced his complaints to God, who, after all, permitted this to happen. Job wanted answers. (Again, can you relate?) However, as he complained to God, part of his argument turned into a sort of praise. He continued to acknowledge his Creator God, even as he argued his case: "You formed me with your hands; you made me… You guided my conception and formed me in the womb. You clothed me with skin and flesh, and you knit my bones and sinews together" (Job 10:8a, 10-11, NLT). Job praised God that he was knitted together in his mother's womb, crafted by His very hands.

This truth that God has intimately created each of us is repeated over and over again in Scripture. Moses received firsthand knowledge of God as Creator when the LORD appeared to him in a burning bush:

Moses said to the LORD, "Pardon your servant, Lord. I have
never been eloquent, neither in the past nor since you have
spoken to your servant. I am slow of speech and tongue."
The LORD said to him, "Who gave human beings their mouths?
Who makes them deaf or mute? Who gives them sight or makes
them blind? Is it not I, the LORD? Now go; I will help you speak
and will teach you what to say." (Exodus 4:10-12)

The Lord was making it clear to Moses that He created him on purpose, for a purpose. Even with Moses' lack of eloquence, his purpose would be fulfilled for God's glory.

Many years later, Moses recalled his encounter with God the Creator in a song he wrote for the Israelites. He knew that his life would soon be over and that the Israelites would rebel in his absence. The song was to serve as both a chastisement and a warning. Moses calls out their foolishness: "Is he not your Father, your Creator, who made you and formed you?" (Deuteronomy 32:6b). Moses wanted the Israelites to forever remember God was their Creator, so he put in a song to make it easier for them. (You know, to get stuck in their heads like that song your kids sing just once, then your toes are tapping all day to the beat.) Afterward, Moses told them, "Take to heart all the words I have solemnly declared to you this day…They are not just idle words for you, they are your life" (Deuteronomy 32:46-47b). These words can bring life to you, too.

Later, Isaiah wrote that the people of Israel were formed and made for God's glory (Isaiah 43:7). Paul also touched on the theme of creation and purpose in Ephesians 2:10: "For we are God's handiwork, created in Christ Jesus to do good works, which God prepared in advance for us to do." We've been created through Him and for Him (Colossians 1:16), and in Him we live and move and have our being (Acts 17:28). Our purpose can only be realized when we first acknowledge that we've been designed by Him and then yield our lives to the Designer.

Since God is the One who bound together each of the three billion characters of your specific DNA sequence, He's the One who is responsible for your physical appearance. He put each of your five million hair follicles in place and has each hair numbered on your head (Luke 12:7). You are not an accident. Your face, your body, and your personality were melded together to make you into His unique treasure. He breathed His own breath of life into your nostrils (Genesis 2:7). Paul tells us in Acts 17:24-25 that the God who made the world and everything in it, the Lord of Heaven and earth, is the same God that gives you life and breath and everything else. Know this: The God who set the stars in the sky, who commands the raging ocean waters, and who keeps the world spinning, has also intimately created each one of us!

Because He is trustworthy, you can believe Him when He says He handcrafted you in His image. Humans are the *only* thing He created which bear His image, and He called His creation "very good" (Genesis 1:31). We're a reflection of Him, and we have the opportunity to share His likeness with the world. We all fall short of His glory because of sin, and we can't reflect His image perfectly. However, He chose to leave His imprint on us. We are being renewed into His likeness day by day.

As we get more familiar with our Creator, we become more like Him. We take off our old sinful nature, just as we would a sweater covered in spilled coffee or baby spit-up. We replace it with a clean, dry, and better smelling sweater. Our new nature consists of compassion, kindness, humility, gentleness, patience, forgiveness, and love (Colossians 3:8-14). We can choose to dress in clothing from God's wardrobe, looking more and more like our Creator every day.

My granny used to be an avid cross-stitcher. I remember mornings at her house from my childhood. I'd wake up to find her on the sofa, bent over a piece of Aida cloth illuminated by her craft light, her cup of coffee cooling on the table beside her. She didn't like the easy designs! If you know anything about cross stitching, you know it's a labor of love. Each square inch of those complicated designs takes about an hour to stitch. My granny stitched a birth announcement for each of my sons. We matted, framed, and hung them on prominent walls in our home where we could appreciate them daily. When we moved across the country, I treasured these birth announcements too much to allow the movers to pack them. I carefully wrapped them and transported them myself in my own car to our new house.

The teddy bears and cartoon jungle animals adorning these birth announcements aren't what I love most about them. It's the fact that those tiny x's have been hand-stitched and given to me by someone who loves me dearly. Our bodies are the same. They're a personal gift from the Lover of our souls, stitched together with His own hands.

When we compare ourselves with other women, we aren't showing appreciation towards what God calls "good" (Genesis 1:31). We were never meant to compare ourselves to airbrushed porn stars because we have not been airbrushed! Even if we did have the "ideal" body (which varies culturally, historically, and geographically) or the combined physical attributes of all the beautiful women at the gym, our hearts would still be discontent without a full understanding of God's truth.

Remember that the Bible describes Satan as "the father of lies" in John 8:44. He will take every opportunity to cause you to doubt your value and identity. Instead of being defined by falsehoods, we can use God's Word to proclaim the truth. We have been intricately molded, shaped, and designed. He's given us differences and unique traits for a reason. Letting our imagination carry us into comparison kills joy and gratitude. This causes us to focus on what we don't have, instead of all we do. Rather than comparison, let's live contently in the bodies that were designed for us, showing the glory of our Creator God.

God is good, and everything He creates is good. In this season of deep grief and suffering, may you remember and take comfort in the truth that you are the Creator's best work. You are His first choice. I pray the next time you look in a mirror, you see the reflection of Jesus.

Prayer for Today

Father, when I am comparing myself to others and feeling insecure, remind me I am Yours. May my body and my life reflect Your glory.

Questions to Ponder

1. Read Genesis 1:26-31. What distinguishes humans from the rest of God's creation? What does it indicate about the Creator's heart for you?

2. What characteristics and/or talents has the Lord given you? How have you been able to use these gifts to glorify to the Creator? What good works did God prepare just for you?

3. What are your favorite parts about yourself? What are the parts you don't especially love? How would your perspective change if you decided to view yourself from God the Father's eyes? Write a script of what God would say about you.

Chapter 10

He Knows Me
(And Has a Plan!)

"You know when I sit and when I rise; you perceive my thoughts from afar. You discern my going out and my lying down; you are familiar with all my ways."

Psalm 139:2-3

I used to wear a silver bar necklace with the word "forgiven" engraved on it. I wanted a daily visual reminder—not too flashy but not too common—of who I was in Christ. Originally, I wore it hoping people would notice and ask me about it, giving me an opportunity to share about God's love. However, I did the exact opposite in my most memorable exchange regarding the necklace. During my annual physical, my doctor saw it as she was doing my breast exam.

"What's that about on your necklace?" she asked.

I told her.

"Hmm, if I had one, it would probably say 'guilty,'" she said.

I longed to explain to her how my Jesus had come to take away feelings like that, but I was naked from the waist up, and she had three more patients to see before lunch. I hesitated, and the opportunity slipped away before I had a chance to button my top. I wore that necklace for a long time after that, but it became more of a personal reminder that I had been forgiven, rather than a ministry tool.

John 4:1-30 tells the story of Jesus talking with a Samaritan woman at a well. Going against cultural norms, He met her in the noonday heat and spoke with her about an assortment of things: living water, husbands, and places of worship. At the end of their conversation Jesus revealed His identity to her by affirming He was the Messiah—one of the only times He did this in Scripture.

For this Samaritan woman, a Savior only for the Jews would be of no use to her. However, Jesus made it clear that He had come to save her, too.

Jesus was fully aware of everything the Samaritan woman had ever done, how she'd had five husbands and was now living with her boyfriend. He didn't shame her or make her feel guilty, but He didn't affirm her in her sin. He did speak the truth in love, letting her know that she was known and accepted. It was mercy. No longer burdened and weighed down by her sins, she left her water jug (and her shame!) at the well to go back into town to share about Jesus. The Bible says many Samaritans ended up believing that day.

Jesus knows us intimately, just like He knew the woman at the well. He knows how we've sinned, and the guilt we carry. Like many other women who have been betrayed, I struggled with wondering if the betrayal was a punishment for the way I had treated my husband in the past.

Was it a consequence of me acting out my bitterness and resentment towards him for being gone all the time due to work? I replayed the past in my mind, trying to pinpoint the areas where I could have done better. I regretted the harsh words I'd said to him and felt shame for ignoring his needs. In a way, I started to carry a burden of guilt that I shouldn't have. I was tempted during these times to mark myself "guilty" instead of "forgiven." It took time (and a healthy dose of counseling!) for me to separate my sin from Will's sin.

Now, I realize that under no circumstances did any of my actions *cause* my husband to be unfaithful. This is a lie from the Enemy. All the same, your husband made his choice regardless of your sin. The Enemy is known as the accuser, and we need to be aware of his schemes (Revelation 12:10; 1 Peter 5:8). He would like nothing better than to pour on the guilt and watch you suffer under the weight of the past. You did not – could not – *cause* your husband to be unfaithful. We must be cautious to not pick up and willingly carry the blame for their betrayals.

Just because my husband's sin was front and center didn't mean I didn't have my own sins which separately needed to be addressed. Infidelity is one example of our deep and recurrent tendency to sin. It also shows the limitlessness of God's grace. It's easy, however, to take such a "big" sin and use it to keep the limelight on the other person. Jesus says in Matthew 7:3-5:

> *Why do you look at the speck of sawdust in your brother's eye*
> *and pay no attention to the plank in your own eye? How can*
> *you say to your brother, "Let me take the speck out of your eye,"*
> *when all the time there is a plank in your own eye? You*
> *hypocrite, first take the plank out of your own eye, and then you*
> *will see clearly to remove the speck from your brother's eye.*

Just like my necklace reminded me, I am fully known, AND fully forgiven—past, present, and future. That's the great thing about mercy and grace—we don't deserve them and can't earn them. Romans 3:23-24 says, "For all have sinned and fall short of the glory of God, and all are justified freely by His grace through the redemption that came by Christ Jesus." When Christ announced with His last breath, "It is finished," in John 19:30, it was like Him saying, "Your sins have been paid in full. You are completely forgiven."

When God looks at me, He doesn't see defects, flaws, and stains. He sees me covered in the blood of the spotless Lamb. Just as the Samaritan woman could walk away from the well, freed from her burdens of guilt and shame, I can rest assured knowing I am fully known and fully forgiven.

Fully known yet fully forgiven is a theme in the story of another well-known biblical character: David. Often in Sunday school, David is portrayed as a cute shepherd boy, wearing his white robe and playing his harp. Children will learn the stories of David's early life to show them that when God is with them, they can accomplish great things, like slaying giants and defeating the bad guys. Some of the stories from later in David's life are less popular in Sunday school: the stories of him committing adultery and murder. I have often thought about how weird it is that despite his pride and blatant sins, God calls David a man after His own heart.

David had been hand-picked by God to lead the nation of Israel as its king. He was an excellent king who led with faith and was committed to following God's law, except when he had sex with the beautiful Bathsheba, knowing she was married. When David found out she was pregnant with his child, he unsuccessfully tried to cover it up. When that didn't work, he had Bathsheba's husband killed. The Bible doesn't skirt around the ugliness of sin and failure. David's story is there, written plainly for all generations to read. We don't need to dive into the effects and consequences of betrayal in this story. It's not new to our culture or our generation. We've all felt it. It messes with God's design and purpose for marriage and sex, culminating in dire consequences.

What we can focus on is that God knew David's heart. When David was confronted by the prophet Nathan regarding these sins, he acknowledged his wrongdoing and immediately repented. In 2 Samuel 12:13, Nathan tells David, "The LORD has taken away your sin." David was a man after God's own heart because he loved and worshiped God, repented of his sins quickly, and constantly turned to God for help.

If you are struggling with harmful thoughts of guilt or blame, ask God to search your heart. You can borrow David's prayer from Psalm 139:23-24: "Search me, God, and know my heart; test me and know my anxious thoughts. See if there is any offensive way in me, and lead me in the way everlasting." God will purify your heart, just ask.

If the Holy Spirit reveals something that you need to repent of, be brave; God's on your side. Read Psalm 103:8-12:

The LORD is compassionate and gracious,
slow to anger, abounding in love.
He will not always accuse,
nor will he harbor his anger forever;
he does not treat us as our sins deserve
or repay us according to our iniquities.
For as high as the heavens are above the earth,
so great is his love for those who fear him;
as far as the east is from the west,
so far has he removed our transgressions from us.

You may have heard this verse explained this way: if you were to place your finger on a globe and slide it north, you'd eventually get to the top of the globe and head south. However, if you place your finger on the equator and slide to the east as you spin the globe, you will keep going east. As long as you keep going the same direction along the equator, you will never go west. The distance between east and west is therefore unlimited. God's forgiveness is also unlimited. He removes our sins so far from us that we can't even comprehend the distance. You don't have to wear your guilt! When we confess our sins, they are erased (Isaiah 43:25; 1 John 1:9).

In addition to knowing our sins, our Lord knows how we feel. Jesus is fully acquainted with our hardships because He was human! Isaiah prophesied about Jesus' humanity before He was even born: "He was despised and rejected by mankind, a man of suffering, and familiar with pain. Like one from whom people hide their faces he was despised and we held him in low esteem" (Isaiah 53:3).

Jesus felt the emotions that you are experiencing right now: anger, when He found people using the temple as a marketplace (John 2:14-16); grief, when He saw Mary weeping over the death of her brother (John 11:35); exhaustion and the desire to be alone (Matthew 14:13); and anguish over knowing the suffering He would soon endure (Luke 22:44). In Mark 14:34, Jesus even says, "My soul is overwhelmed with sorrow to the point of death." He knows your sorrow. He empathizes.

If we're experiencing infertility, we don't seek advice from our coworker who has seven kids and is expecting her eighth. Instead, we'll go to our neighbor who has walked the same journey of uncertainty and extreme sadness. If there's a death in our family, we go to the women in our lives who have suffered the same grievous loss. They might not know the words to say, but they know how to just be there with us. Just the same, when we're processing a betrayal, we need a trusted confidant who understands the confusion, the conflicting emotions, and the anguish we're experiencing. These people might be hard to find. We don't all sport a bright yellow letter "B" for "betrayed" on our right shoulder. We might be tempted to unload to the first available person, but it's important to pray for discernment and listen to His guidance for finding support. While you wait for God to guide you to the right people—the ones who will pray with you, avoid gossip, protect your confidence, and encourage you in your faith—know that you can go to Jesus. You can take your grief, sadness, and anger to Him in prayer, asking Him to help you walk through it. He understands betrayal.

He knows you intimately and knows how the affair or addiction has disrupted your entire life. He also has a plan for you to make it through this. He can (and will) accomplish His plans, even in your worst-case scenario. The Israelites were seeing their worst-case scenario played out as they were carried away into captivity by the Babylonians. God promised them, "For I know the plans I have for you…plans to prosper you and not to harm you, plans to give you hope and a future" (Jeremiah 29:11). God had arranged a plan, and His children, the Israelites, would not have to live in captivity forever.

People (even well-meaning Christians) sometimes take this verse out of context. They use it to tell themselves that God has plans for their financial prosperity, plans to heal every sickness or disease, and plans to make their future totally successful. In our case, we might wrongly assume that "prospering" includes having a porn-free marriage by Friday, seeing our husbands repent of their unfaithfulness, or having them beg for our forgiveness. However, this thought process isn't aligned with the verse in context.

Jeremiah 29:11 doesn't promise that everything is going to work out to make us happy. The Lord prefaced His assurance of prosperity and hope by saying that the Israelites would be in exile for seventy years before they would receive their freedom. The truth of this passage is this: God knows us intimately and has a plan for us, even if that plan takes longer than we'd like. While God's plan isn't something we always understand or even see, we can know that the details of our lives are safe in His hand. We have hope and a future.

When we feel trapped at the climax of our story, afraid there's no resolution, God can see one. He has a plan. God sent His Son into the world to offer forgiveness of sins and an eternal relationship with Him. God knew we would need rescuing from our lives of sin and was able to come up with the grandest, most loving plan of all time. We can trust Him with what we are going through now.

Prayer for Today

Lord, thank You for knowing me inside and out. You love me no matter what I've done. Rather than distancing Yourself from me because of my sin, You draw me closer. I do not take Your forgiveness for granted. I know that You are familiar with every emotion I feel because You once lived in this imperfect world. You know every detail of the story that's unfolding. Help me to trust even more in Your plan for my life.

Questions to Ponder

1. There are many beautiful encounters between Jesus and women in the Bible. Read John 8:1-12. Jesus knew this woman and her sin, yet He showed her grace. How does He call her into the light? What does this story mean to you?

2. In what ways does it bring you comfort to know that Jesus also experienced anger, grief, exhaustion, anguish, and sorrow? What is your response to His invitation to come to Him in Matthew 11:28?

3. What unknowns regarding your future currently concern you? How is your relationship with God impacted when you choose to believe He has a plan for your good? As you wait on His timing, how can you show Him you trust Him?

Chapter 11

Take Shelter!

"The L*ord* *is my rock, my fortress, and my savior; my God is my rock, in whom I find protection. He is my shield, the power that saves me, and my place of safety."*

Psalm 18:2, NLT

I've seen a photo online of a father on a battlefield with his daughter. A war rages around them. Flaming arrows fly at them. In one hand, he holds a shield above himself and his child, while in the other, he offers flowers to his daughter. The child isn't focused on the attack, only on the beauty of the flowers. This image was how I pictured my Heavenly Father during the months I sorted through my grief.

I wasn't oblivious to the war around us, complete with anger, temptation, fear, bitterness, and a desire for revenge. There were half-truths, partial disclosures, crying, and screaming. The headaches, sleepless nights, nausea, and lack of focus were overwhelming. My life depended on moment-by-moment prayer. In all of this, I knew God was actively protecting me. Proverbs 30:5 tells us that He is a shield to those who take refuge in Him. I longed for safety, and under His shield I found protection.

One of my favorite stories of God's mighty protection is written in 2 Kings 6:8-18. At the time, Aram was at war with Israel. God's prophet, Elisha, could accurately predict the strategic moves the king of Aram would make. Elisha would update the king of Israel frequently with warnings. He'd say, "Beware of passing that place, because the Arameans are going down there" (verse 9). The king of Israel heeded these warnings and avoided conflict with Aram. At first, the king of Aram suspected there was a traitor in his army. His officers informed him it was not a traitor, but a prophet exposing their position. One of the officers even said, "Elisha, the prophet who is in Israel, tells the king of Israel the very words you speak in your bedroom" (verse 12b). I can imagine the king gritting his teeth in anger, his face turning fiery red. How much time and effort had gone into his planning, just to have his secrets "leaked" to the enemy!

After learning about Elisha, the king of Aram sent a strong fighting force (of what I imagine were his mightiest warriors) to capture Elisha. When Elisha's servant woke up that morning and saw the enemy surrounding them, he panicked. "Oh no, my lord! What shall we do?" (verse 15).

Elisha told his servant not to fear: "Those who are with us are more than those who are with them" (verse 16). Elisha prayed that his servant's eyes would be opened to the powerful protection of the Lord. Understandably, the servant's eyes were fixed on the very big and very real problem of the Aramean soldiers surrounding them. After all, if Elisha was captured, then the servant would be dead meat, too.

The Lord opened the servant's eyes to see the angel army that was protecting him and Elisha. He saw that the hills were full of horses and chariots of fire. The enemy looked big, but they were completely outnumbered by God's army! The Bible says God struck the entire enemy army with blindness, and the fight was over before it even started. No opposition stands a chance when we call upon the mighty protection of God.

Psalm 18:2 (NLT) says, "The LORD is my rock, my fortress, and my savior; my God is my rock, in whom I find protection. He is my shield, the power that saves me, and my place of safety."

Placing your trust in God for refuge doesn't mean bad things will stop happening. It also doesn't mean your husband will immediately repent and want a faithful marriage. There are so many different ways your path of marriage might head, and no matter which path, there's a difficult journey ahead. Even amidst your loneliness, tears, and apprehension, you will always be under the shelter of His wings. As Moses blessed the twelve tribes of Israel, he said of Benjamin, "Let the beloved of the Lord rest secure in him, for he shields him all day long, and the one the Lord loves rests between His shoulders" (Deuteronomy 33:12). What a sweet picture, to be resting between the shoulders of the Lord.

Taking shelter under His shield helps us keep a firm grasp on the truth that we are protected from the enemy's attacks. The Enemy will hurl spears of temptation at us, like the thought to defame our husbands on social media or the opportunity to gossip about our husbands to our friends. God's words of wisdom help us to choose not to repay evil for evil.

When the arrows of fear fly—and they will countless times of day—know God's presence is with you. He promises this in Joshua 1:9: "Be strong and courageous! Do not be afraid or discouraged. For I am with you wherever you go."

With the Lord's prompting, one of my friends told me I should write down all of my fears. I decided to oblige and opened my journal to the next blank page. At the top, I wrote the date, October 6, 2021, and titled it "Fears." My fears ranged from, "I'll get bitter again," to "I'll never be able to trust him." As I was writing fear number sixteen on the bottom line of the page, I noticed the verse printed on the margin: "God has said, 'Never will I leave you; never will I forsake you.' So we say with confidence, 'The Lord is my helper; I will not be afraid' (Hebrews 13:5-6a)." Coincidence? I think not! God had reserved this page for my fears. Now written in purple ink, I offered my fears to Him so He would guide me through them.

All my fears were things that *might* happen. I used so much brain power and wasted so much time stressing over them. Now, as I look back at my journal entry, I can see that many of the things I was afraid of never happened. My story isn't your story, though.

Maybe your fears are different, or they've come true. Perhaps your husband has abandoned you, and you're sorting through a stack of legal paperwork, fearful of how you'll support yourself. Maybe he hasn't decided to seek help. Perhaps he is continuing to indulge in destructive behaviors, and you fear what your children might see when they visit him. Maybe situations you never thought of fearing are now unfolding. Perhaps he contracted a sexually transmitted disease (STD) when he cheated on you, and you just found out he gave it to you. Even when you are walking through the scariest of times, know that God never leaves. Just like He promised Joshua, His shield is over you, wherever you go. You are walking under His protection.

When depression and anxiety bombard us and we find it impossible to get out of bed, He tells us, "Give all of your worries and cares to God, for he cares about you." (1 Peter 5:7, NLT). He prevents us from being crushed by the burdens we shoulder. He picks them up, freeing us to walk a little lighter.

Weakness and despair will be thrown in our direction like grenades. When we feel like death would be less work than walking through the enemy's minefield of more pain, doubt, and triggers, we can read Psalm 46. The words of the psalmist will fortify us, reminding us God Almighty remains our refuge and strength. He will send help in times of trouble.

Martin Luther's most famous hymn, *A Mighty Fortress is Our God*, is based on this psalm. It is said that when Luther faced difficulty and danger, he would resort to singing this song. The second stanza resonates most deeply with me. We cannot fight this battle in our weariness and despair, but Jesus Christ, our Lord Almighty, is on our side, and He will win.

Did we in our own strength confide,
Our striving would be losing,
Were not the right Man on our side,
The Man of God's own choosing.
You ask who that may be?
Christ Jesus, it is He;
Lord Sabaoth His name,
From age to age the same;
And He must win the battle.

Over time, I developed a feeling of peace. I knew even though my husband might not choose to repent and protect me from any more hurt, I had a Father who was the perfect protector. Jesus didn't just risk His life for me, He surrendered it. He gave His very last breath to protect me from an eternity in Hell. He endured the most torturous punishment and death so that my future would be protected and secure. Jesus is who I need to be running to every day for refuge. His shield is my place of safety. Psalm 91:1 promises us, "Those who live in the shelter of the Most High will rest in the shadow of the Almighty." Here, under his protection, there is beauty.

Prayer for Today

Lord, thank You that I don't need to be afraid of the battle because I am at rest between Your shoulders. Your shield of protection covers me. You are my refuge and my fortress. Thank You that I can trust You to protect my soul. Remind me to bring each and every fear to You.

Questions to Ponder

1. What is your first response when facing triggers, anxiety, or distress? How can praying calm your heart?

2. What "arrows of fear" are currently flying at you? How does it impact you to know that God's shield is bigger and stronger than the situations you fear?

3. Where have you seen the beauty of God's protection in your life?

Chapter 12

Abba

"If you, then, though you are evil, know how to give good gifts to your children, how much more will your Father in heaven give good gifts to those who ask him!"

Matthew 7:11

I was a labor and delivery nurse for fifteen years, honored to help welcome hundreds of new lives into the world. Like most L&D nurses, my favorite part of the job was watching a newborn baby meet its family for the first time.

Often, when things were running smoothly in the delivery room, my eyes would fix on the dad, to see how he would respond to the birth. I was usually able to get away with staring for a long time, since he would never be paying attention to me. Usually, he'd be leaning over his wife's leg, watching the birth.

He'd been waiting for this moment for months, and now it was happening right before his eyes. As the baby's head would rotate to the side, the dad would be the first one to see his baby. For me, the most satisfying part of the pushing stage was watching the father's expression change the first time he saw his child's face. Most of the time, he would sigh or gasp in delight. Sometimes he would laugh or cry. Occasionally, he'd collapse, and I'd have to pick his limp body up off the floor. There was always a smile. There's nothing in the world quite like watching a man's heart turn to mush in a matter of seconds. This was the moment he'd been waiting for, and he would remember it for the rest of his life. He had just become a father. The full reality of that had just hit him.

These were incredible memories for me, but the reality is that many of these dads won't end up living in the same home as their child. The US Census Bureau estimated in 2022 that the United States had 10.9 million one-parent families, 80 percent of which were single-mother households.[2] If I'm doing my math correctly, that means there are nearly 9 million households in the United States without a dad. When you consider that these households can have multiple children, the number of fatherless children is staggering. While many dads do remain invested in their children's lives, there are way too many children in the United States without a strong fatherly influence.

I understand this is a sensitive topic for many people. Perhaps, like me, you had a father who chose to dismiss the God-given gift of fatherhood. From my earliest years, my dad was more interested in alcohol than he was in his family. His alcoholism didn't allow him to keep a job or fulfill many of his responsibilities as a father. By the time I was a pre-teen, he was addicted to drugs. Living in the home with him was unsafe, and he and my mom went through an ugly divorce. There are so many facets to alcohol and drug addiction, but children don't understand all of them. Nor should they have to. In my thirteen-year-old mind, it was clear: my dad didn't choose me.

As I processed my husband's betrayal, feelings of rejection bubbled up that I hadn't felt for years. During one of our first marriage counseling sessions, the counselor asked about our families of origin. I finally connected the newer feelings of rejection I had to those from my childhood, even though I hated that he had asked about my growing up years.

---

[2] US Census Bureau. "Census Bureau Releases New Estimates on America's Families and Living Arrangements." Census.gov, November 17, 2022. https://www.census.gov/newsroom/press-releases/2022/americas-families-and-living-arrangements.html.

I wanted to focus on the current problem, not the one I had kept successfully stuffed down for twenty years. I knew how what we experience in our formative years can shape the way we relate to people, heal from hurts, and view the world, but I didn't want to connect those dots. I feared if I did, the blame for the infidelity would somehow be put on me, and that wasn't fair. I'd heard people comment about "women with daddy issues," and I'd also heard people talk negatively about victims of infidelity, saying things like, "She picked a man who is just like her dad. What did she expect?" I wasn't interested in including my dad in our current conflict, even though the counselor's probing was making it unavoidable.

I saw myself rejected like a piece of trash, thrown from a car window by a careless teen. I felt like there were two clear choices: me or another woman. We were actively working on restoring our relationship, but I thought of the past times when he hadn't chosen me.

How could I have kept Will's attention better? Was I not providing something at home that caused him to seek it elsewhere? What had I neglected in our relationship? How could I have prevented him from straying? Why didn't he choose me? I asked myself these questions repeatedly.

Friend, if we were speaking in person, I'd cup your face in my hands and look straight into your eyes. I would tell you this: "You are in no way responsible for the choice your husband made to step outside of your marriage for sexual or emotional fulfillment."

In the same way that I could never have prevented my dad from choosing alcohol and drugs over his family, I could never have prevented my husband from the temptations he indulged in and the sins he chose. I want to remind you, instead, of the many ways God the Father chooses us, treasures us, and cherishes us. They were what I needed to be reminded of back then.

In Deuteronomy 7:6, God speaks through Moses to share with the Israelites just how much they meant to Him: "For you are a people holy to the LORD your God. The LORD your God has chosen you out of all the peoples on the face of the earth to be his people, his treasured possession."

I love that phrase, "treasured possession." It reminds me of a newborn baby being taken home from the hospital. Her father isn't going to let anything bad happen to her. He has installed the car seat base in the back seat so tightly that it will take a pair of hedge trimmers to get it undone (not that I know from experience). He's checked and rechecked that the car seat straps are snug, but not too snug (having exactly one finger-breadth of space between them and the baby's chest). The buckle is lined up straight across the nipple line, and the cushioned head roll is in its proper position. He carries her out of the hospital, careful not to swing the carrier, and gently places her car seat into its base. He then begins the long, cautious drive home. He's never driven this slowly before, but he's got precious cargo now. This new father only met his baby a day or two ago, but she is already his most treasured possession.

If an earthly father, who is imperfect, is capable of this level of care and concern, how much more is our Heavenly Father capable of cherishing us? God set us apart as His treasured possession before we were even conceived (Jeremiah 1:5). We haven't been left abandoned as we grapple with rejection. Our Heavenly Father reigns as Sovereign King of the World, and as daughters of the King, we have full access to Him anytime we want. He is intimately involved and concerned with every detail of our lives. His Word invites us to, "See what great love the Father has lavished on us, that we should be called children of God! And that is what we are!" (1 John 3:1a-b).

Ephesians 3:12 tells us that we can approach God with confidence. He invites us—the rejected, the unchosen, and the burdened—to ask, seek, and knock (Matthew 7:7). Every challenge, hurt, and pain can be an opportunity to turn to God to seek His comfort. When we prioritize going to Him in prayer, we're showing that we trust Him with our hurts. He's honored to be available (Psalm 147:11).

During my months of sadness, I discovered how easily accessible God is. Not one single prayer went unheard, and not one cry for help went unanswered. I told Him how I truly felt: *God, vengeance is Yours. Please repay Will tenfold for what he's done.* I also got creative: *God, if Will is tempted to go someplace or be with someone he shouldn't, please give him uncontrollable diarrhea.*

I've seen lots of paintings of Jesus carrying a lamb over His shoulders. I've also heard stories of shepherds in the old days who would break the legs of their wayward sheep. They would then carry them for miles to teach them to stay with the fold. I prayed that God would allow me to be the one to help crack Will's femurs. He needed to be carried for a while.

While my prayers were only halfway serious, God saw beyond my anger to the hurt underneath them. Since God is all-knowing, He can't be surprised or shocked. He knows our hearts. Before a word is on our tongue, He knows it completely (Psalm 139:4). In His grace, He was also patient and kind in my less faithful moments: *Lord, I don't like what You're doing here, and I don't believe there is any good purpose in it.* He was there when I would say three words of a prayer, then be bombarded by an evil thought I'd entertain for a while. When I went back to Him, He was still there, patiently waiting for me to talk with Him.

Won't you try it? A simple prayer could start like this: "Father, I know You desire time to sit with me and console my broken heart. When I'm alone, feeling rejected and abandoned, remind me that You're always with me. Help me to remember to seek You every time I am hurting."

Sometimes we don't even have words when we take our pain to Him. As our Abba Father, He's big enough, strong enough, and kind enough to allow us to pour out our hearts to Him, no matter what we sound like. David prayed this way in Psalm 38: "I am feeble and utterly crushed; I groan in anguish of heart. All my longings lie open before you, Lord; my sighing is not hidden from you" (verses 8-9). God is never too busy, tired, or distracted to listen. He knows what we need before we even ask. Not only does our Good Father accept our kind, selfless, and contrite prayers, but also He welcomes the raw, emotional words of a downcast soul. He cares for you (1 Peter 5:7).

As I began to run to the Lord more quickly and frequently, I developed a new closeness with Him. Any man can be a father, and any girl can be a daughter, but a thriving father-daughter relationship takes time, intentionality, priority, and effort. The point wasn't to get what I wanted. The point was to spend time with the One I love. The more time I spent with Him, the more I enjoyed His presence, and the more I got to know His character.

It was during this season that I began a new habit of praying continually, like Paul encouraged the Thessalonians to do in 1 Thessalonians 5:17. This was especially helpful when intrusive thoughts entered my mind. "Lord, take it away," was often whispered, and a quick, "Help me, God," was pretty common. Prayer wasn't always my first reaction to a new stressor, but I got there eventually.

He really did answer, even my short, desperate prayers. I'd always known that God answers prayer in His will, in His way, and in His timing. I'd been a Christian my entire life, but now, I was seeing Him work in such amazing ways that I started really noting the answers.

Jesus spoke about His Father's heart in Matthew 7:9-11: "Which of you, if your son asks for bread, will give him a stone? Or if he asks for a fish, will give him a snake? If you, then, though you are evil, know how to give good gifts to your children, how much more will your father in heaven give good gifts to those who ask him!"

He wants to bless His kids' socks off! Every good and perfect gift is from above, coming down from our Father of the Heavenly Lights (James 1:17).

One answered prayer stands out in my mind, probably because of the smoke. At the time, many things around our house triggered painful memories and feelings in me. I asked the Lord to help Will be more sensitive to my triggers and sympathetic to my feelings. A few of my friends were praying for the same thing, but so far, walking around my home was making me think about betrayal at every turn. A memento from one of his work trips hung on the wall, and it brought up particularly negative feelings for me.

God spoke to Will's heart. One night, when I got home from my support group, Will asked if the memento bothered me. I told him that it did. Immediately, he took it off the wall and marched outside. He tossed it into the fire pit, then threw a match on it. The smoke wafted into the open window of my second story bedroom, like the fragrance of a praise offering. Gratitude filled my heart. The Lord had answered my prayer in a literal blaze of glory!

God reminded me through that incident that He can (and will) answer prayers in all kinds of ways! This showed me the truth of this verse: "He who did not spare his own Son, but gave him up for us all— how will he not also, along with him, graciously give us all things?" (Romans 8:32).

Just because God is sometimes silent doesn't mean He doesn't care or isn't capable. His answers can be immediate, but they can also take time. Either way, His timing is perfect. Our good Father holds all knowledge. If He doesn't give us exactly what we want when we want it, it's because His plan is better. He loves us too much to give us only a temporary fix when there's a better solution down the road. If they could, our kids would eat ice cream for dinner every night of the week. As their moms, we know it's not good for them. We can trust that when the answer is "No" or "Wait," it's the most caring answer for now.

Have you trusted the Lord with your life? Romans 10:9 assures us that salvation is available to all: "If you declare with your mouth, 'Jesus is Lord,' and believe in your heart that God raised him from the dead, you will be saved." As a good Father, God doesn't overpower your free will and make you choose Him. When you declare the risen Jesus as King over your life, you will be making the best decision of your life. You won't regret giving your life into the hands of the Perfect Father.

You don't have to clean up your life before you go to Him; you can come just as you are.

Acts 3:19 says, "Repent, then, and turn to God, so that your sins may be wiped out, that times of refreshing may come from the Lord." Let Him know you don't want to live another day without Him as Lord of your life. Any time is a good time to surrender your life into the hands of God, but why not now? After you do, tell someone. Get connected with a church family who will celebrate this decision with you and encourage you in your new faith.

Perhaps you have surrendered your life to the Lord, but currently feel like your relationship with Him is strained. Maybe it's been a long time since you've talked with Him. Don't worry! Open your Bible to the story of the prodigal son in Luke 15:11-32 to see how God responds to a child who returns to Him. Jesus used this parable to teach His followers about how God is a forgiving, gracious Father.

The story goes like this: A father had two sons and his younger son asks for his inheritance early. He wants to see the world and party. His father obliges, and the son leaves town. He squanders the money on wild living and has to take a job feeding pigs. Famine hits the land, and he's so desperate for food that he wants to eat the pig slop. The starvation makes him come to his senses. He decides to return to His father, with the intention of working as a hired servant.

"But while he was still a long way off, his father saw him and was filled with compassion for him; he ran to his son, threw his arms around him and kissed him" (Luke 15:20b). The father welcomes him back. He gives him a robe, ring, and sandals. He throws a party to celebrate, and says, "For this son of mine was dead and is alive again; he was lost and is found" (Luke 15:24a). God the Father is waiting for you. He is ready for you, with His arms open wide.

The Father's heart is grieved that you, His treasured daughter, are having to walk through this journey of hurt and sorrow. There's a tear-jerking video on YouTube® of the athlete Derek Redmond running in the 1992 Olympics. About 15 seconds after the start of the 400-meter race, Derek seriously injures his leg and collapses onto the rubber track. Desperate to finish the race, he gets up and begins limping toward the finish line, grimacing more and more with each step. His father, who is in the stands, sees the anguish in his son's face and runs down to his son, breaking through security! He comes to Derek's side, and Derek leans on him for support. They walk together to the finish line.

You might feel like Derek, experiencing excruciating pain and disappointment over what's happened. God sees your pain and the heaviness in your soul. He's right beside you, walking every step of the way with you.

This fallen world isn't the world He intended for His children to live in. He didn't intend for sin to wreak havoc on our lives and steal our joy. He did all He could, while still allowing free will, to warn humankind of the ugliness of the knowledge of good and evil. When Adam and Eve ate the fruit and sin entered the world, our land of paradise was transformed into a world with pride, hate, trouble, pain, and death. God was hurt because His children made bad choices in the garden. Likewise, God is hurt because of the adultery, the pornography, the addictions and the lies, just like you are. He has your back, though. He promises something wonderful for His daughters.

You can find it in Philippians 4:6-7: "Do not be anxious about anything, but in every situation, by prayer and petition, with thanksgiving, present your requests to God. And the peace of God, which transcends all understanding, will guard your hearts and your minds in Christ Jesus." God promises that when we bring our requests to Him, His peace will guard us. I encourage you to release your anxieties to Him and, in turn, to receive the peace He will send you. What a beautiful exchange!

Rest assured that His presence is with you, He is holding you steady, and has your name engraved on the palm of His hand (Isaiah 49:16). Your Father treasured you as an infant and watches over you as He sanctifies you into the woman He has called you to be. He will continue to cherish you for eternity. You are His, the cherished daughter of the one-and-only Perfect Father.

Prayer for Today

Father God, I am in awe that You chose me to be adopted into Your family as Your treasured daughter. You are aware of every one of my needs. You never cease to show me compassion. When I struggle with thoughts of rejection, remind me that I am chosen by You. Please take away any of my thoughts that compare You to earthly father figures. You are the only Perfect Father. Thank You for allowing me to be called a daughter of the Most High.

Questions to Ponder

1. When you are suffering, how does it help you to know that God has chosen you, sees you, hears you, has compassion on you, and loves you?

2. When you're feeling forgotten, what truths can you dwell on to remember that God never forgets His children?

3. In what area of life do you hold back instead of approaching God's throne with confidence? How does your perspective change when you understand that you have full access to God through Jesus Christ?

Chapter 13

Life-Giving Oxygen

*"My flesh and my heart may fail, but God is
the strength of my heart and my portion forever."*

Psalm 73:26

One of my favorite reminders of our relationship with Christ is that of an umbilical cord. A plump, healthy segment of umbilical cord might cause some people to gag, but I love them! My enthusiasm for umbilical cords stems from my days as a L&D nurse, when I'd see them every time I went to work.

Back then, most of my work day involved watching the heart rate monitor of my patient's baby. If the baby had an umbilical cord that was really skinny, had two vessels instead of three, or was getting compressed by the labor contractions, then I'd likely see a decreased heart rate. That's because when the umbilical cord isn't functioning optimally, the oxygen flowing to the baby is inadequate. It's a potentially dangerous situation, as the umbilical cord is the baby's lifeline.

In my season of processing the betrayal, I began to understand on a much deeper level how Jesus is my lifeline. Deep, soul-crushing struggles have a way of giving us a new perspective on truths we previously took for granted.

In the past, I had counted on my husband to be my source of help. Not only was he physically stronger than I was, but he had amazing mental strength and resilience. If I needed verbal reassurance I was doing a good job at mothering, he was the perfect one to encourage me in that role. When my feelings were hurt because of something a friend or coworker said, I'd run to him for consolation. He traveled often for his job, and I would call him on the road to ask for advice or share what was happening with the kids. Now, everything had changed.

He was dealing with his own heavy weight of guilt, shame, and confusion. Overwhelmed by what recovery would look like for us, he wasn't sure he was prepared for the work it would involve. I could no longer count on him to be my strength and support in the way he had been for so much of our marriage. However, this ended up being a blessing in disguise. My suffering caused me to turn to Jesus for the strength to persevere and rely solely on Him.

Psalm 73 begins with the psalmist (assumed to be Asaph) writing about how he saw arrogant and wicked people prospering. Wealthy and carefree, they seemed to get away with whatever they wanted. Meanwhile, Asaph tried to do the right thing, but suffered for it. Asaph's perspective changes in the second half of the psalm though: "Whom have I in heaven but you? And earth has nothing I desire besides you. My flesh and my heart may fail, but God is the strength of my heart and my portion forever" (verses 25-26).

God gave Asaph strength as he struggled with circumstances that seemed unfair. He expressed his concerns to God and afterwards acknowledged God was in control. God would deal with the wrongdoers in His time. By the end of the psalm, Asaph says, "But as for me, it is good to be near God" (verse 28a).

This psalm is a good example of how prayer can reset our perspective. Asaph's prayer begins with complaining about an unfair situation, only to end by acknowledging God has given him the strength to endure. Asaph feels closer to God after praying, and we can, too.

Sometimes husbands appear to be unphased by their problematic sexual behaviors, seemingly not reaping the consequences of their actions (like Asaph's acquaintances). This is totally unjust. It's not at all what God had in mind when He designed the marriage covenant. What happened to you was so incredibly unfair. God knows this! There has been unjust suffering in your life because of your husband's wrong choices. You've remained faithful in your marriage but have had to deal with the consequences of a severed relationship. The brokenness of the family weighs on you, and you've been afflicted with wounds no one should ever have to sustain.

The betrayal in your marriage has likely broken your heart. (Sin *should* break our hearts.) It breaks God's heart, too. We can speak with Him honestly about it. God can handle our grief, concerns, questions—even our complaints. We don't shame our children when they approach us with a heavy heart, and our heavenly Father doesn't shame us when we come to Him in prayer. It's okay to cry out to God. It's okay to ask "Why?" and to express our brokenness. There's no sense in wasting time using flowery words or beating around the bush. He knows every word that is on our tongue before we say it (Psalm 139:4).

After you've brought your concerns to God, practice shifting your perspective. Read the second half of Psalm 73 and recite Asaph's words. Give God thanks for His wise guidance and for taking you into glory. Tell Him there is nothing you desire besides Him. Praise Him that even when your heart and flesh fail, He will give you strength. Make this prayer your own. He'll be the One to sustain you, preserve you, and give you strength as you trust in Him today.

If our relationship with God is like an umbilical cord, Jesus is the life-giving oxygen (strength) to our soul. Because He created us, knows us, and sees us, He can accurately determine the right amount of nourishment we need. He delivers it in His perfect timing, in His perfect way. Like an unborn baby depends wholly on his mother for oxygen, we too must depend wholly on God for strength. Of course this comparison doesn't work perfectly, as the Holy Spirit has incredible work to do in our lives as well. But you get the point: Jesus connects us to God.

Jesus teaches us about the source of our strength in the Gospel of John. He says, "I am the vine; you are the branches. If you remain in me and I in you, you will bear much fruit; apart from me you can do nothing" (John 15:5). Jesus says, "Remain in me" six times in the passage. Branches cannot supply their own nourishment any better than a baby in the womb can supply his own oxygen.

Just like an umbilical cord receives life-giving oxygen from a healthy placenta, a vine's branches receive life-giving nutrients and water through the vine. If for any reason the branch is detached from the vine, it will wither and die. Similarly, an umbilical cord cut away from the placenta eventually shrivels up and falls off. We are wholly dependent on God. If we don't abide in Jesus our lives shrivel up and we can't produce fruit. The answer to living a fruitful life rather than a withered one is to remain in Jesus.

We are powerless to do anything without Jesus. God gives us the perfect balance of power and strength to obey Him, even in difficult times. We can display dignity in unfair circumstances because we are abiding in the Vine, soaking in our source of love and grace. We can rejoice in the Lord by putting on a worship song, lifting our praises to Him, and telling him that He is good, even when the situation isn't. We can walk through a life-altering betrayal while still giving honor to God because we're walking with the Holy Spirit, who empowers us to do hard things. We can do all this through Christ, who gives us strength (Philippians 4:13).

Prayer for Today

Lord, my flesh and my heart may fail, but You are the strength of my heart. You are my portion forever. Thank You for being everything I need. My soul is truly satisfied only when I abide in You. Please continue to provide all the strength I need to walk through this difficult season of betrayal.

Questions to Ponder

1. What truths can you remember about God when you need strength and courage? How do they encourage you to walk in obedience?

2. Does it bring you freedom to know that Christ Himself is inviting you to remain in Him? How is He providing strength to you right now?

3. Read John 15:1-8. What "fruit" is the Lord producing in your life as you stay connected to Him, the True Vine?

Chapter 14

Prone to Wander

"Your king will lead you;
the Lord himself will guide you."

Micah 2:13b, NLT

One of the assignments in my betrayal recovery group was to list the things Will's betrayal had stolen from me. The intention of the exercise was to help me pinpoint my specific losses and sort out the resulting emotions with God, not to place blame and harbor resentment. Some losses were only perceived losses, some were temporary, and it took a long time to restore some others. I will never recover from some losses, but I trust God will continue to work out all things for my good.

I wrote out the obvious losses I felt first: trust in my husband, peace of mind, and emotional stability. Later, I added other losses to the list whenever I noticed their impact. Less obvious than my big losses were the smaller losses that snuck up on me and blindsided me with the strength of their force.

One of them was my ability to have fun on our family beach outings. We were living on the coast then, and one of my favorite pastimes was sitting in my beach chair, watching the orange and purple California sunsets. We went at least twice a week, even in the winter.

The boys would play in the sand, and I would relax, the sounds of the waves and wind helping to declutter my mind.

For months after D-Day, when we went to the beach, I realized the "triggers" of bare midriffs, cleavage, and thong bikinis. I would get so frustrated by the women who seemed to be deliberately trying to get men to gawk. Instead of "bouncing my eyes," like men in sexual addiction recovery learn to do, I was the one gawking...in disgust.

Looking back now, I realize these women probably weren't even paying attention to us. They had no interest in stealing my husband. They were probably proud of the hard work they had done at the gym or the weight loss they had accomplished. Maybe they just wanted to get an even tan. However, after other women had stolen what was mine, the seemingly perfect bodies of other women at the beach vexed me. What used to be a relaxing, fun experience was now just disturbing. I grieved losing the ability to enjoy the beauty and peace of God's creation with my family.

I started using social media less, and lost connection with some people as a result. I felt like a fake, like all the happy family experiences I previously posted were counterfeit. Last year's memories would pop up with a photo of our cute, "perfect" Christian family, but now they felt sour. What red flags was I missing during that part of my life? What was Will thinking in this photo? Where was he in that one?

I'd recall when he was traveling and automatically make up a painful story about what he was doing. I felt foolish. How had I not realized I was living in an alternate reality? I used to enjoy sharing photos of our adventures and messaging friends and family. Now, shame compelled me to distance myself from social media altogether, except for obsessively searching for profiles and photos of Will's mistresses.

Important caution for readers: I understand and want the very best for you. Please don't go searching for details on social media. Sometimes memories pop up that we don't anticipate or have no control over, but I'm talking about intentionally rummaging through old posts, filling your mind with unnecessary details about the betrayal. We don't need to know names, hotel locations, restaurants, and colors of dresses or hair. The more details we have, the more opportunities for provocation and triggering we have.

One of my worst discoveries happened when I scrolled through my husband's page and saw a photo collage I had posted to his timeline. I had spent hours searching my hard drives for social media-worthy photos of each boy with his dad. My sweet thoughts of my boys were suddenly hijacked when I noticed the date. This was a weekend we had specifically talked about during one of our counseling sessions. All the recovery and healing up to that point seemed to disappear abruptly. My husband, who was doing well in recovery at the time, was blindsided by my whirlwind of emotions. I was angry all over again, offended, hurt, and disgusted. This situation ruined that date for me. Processing it gets easier with time, as God continues to heal my heart, but I could have prevented the ugliness by not going down that rabbit hole in the first place.

In addition to the other losses, I realized I couldn't donate blood until my labs were repeatedly negative for any sexually transmitted diseases. (Testing is *so* important, and I would encourage you to speak with your doctor about the frequency and types of tests available to you.) As a nurse, I administered lifesaving blood transfusions on occasion, and I valued the opportunity to donate to that cause. I was so frustrated that the opportunity to help save a life was taken from me for a season.

In the subsequent months, I added and subtracted losses from my list. I took "loss of love" and "loss of peace" off the list pretty quickly, as God poured these things generously over me in those months. Even as Will and I were still working on finding love and peace in our marriage, I had been finding a deeper love and peace with God. I haven't added to the list in a while, and I recently reread it. One thing that I noticed: I never lost my way. The Good Shepherd was always there, leading me to follow Him.

The description of Jesus as a shepherd might remind anyone who's been around sheep of the stench that job can entail. Shepherds in Jesus' time lived in the fields full-time, working and sleeping outside. They skipped baths and wore the same dirty clothes and sandals day after day. They were simple men, likely uneducated with no power or influence. David's father Jesse didn't consider that Samuel could possibly anoint his young son as the next king (1 Samuel 16:1-13). David was just out "tending the sheep," as Jesse put it. It was a job that, with proper training, even a child could do.

The relationship between a shepherd and his sheep is really quite sweet. The shepherd knows his sheep well—their shapes and sizes, their sounds, and their personalities—and can identify them from a distance. By watching their individual habits and discovering their temperaments, the shepherd can anticipate their individual needs. The sheep also know their shepherd well. They recognize his face, learn his voice, and follow him. The shepherd's presence reassures them they will be tended, fed, and kept safe because he has done these things repeatedly.

Nowadays, shepherds mark their sheep with an identifier, a notch or tag in their ear. When you and I entrust our lives into the hands of the Good Shepherd, He also marks us with an identifier: the Holy Spirit.

At the moment of conversion, the Holy Spirit indwells us, and we're set apart as God's own. We're adopted as daughters of the King, and we belong to Him forever: "I give them eternal life, and they shall never perish; no one will snatch them out of my hand" (John 10:28). The Lord knows us intimately and never takes His eyes off of us (Job 36:7). We, in turn, spend the rest of our lives getting to know Him, learning His voice, and following His guidance. The more we get to know His character, the more we will trust our lives into the leadership of our Good Shepherd.

The Bible introduces David as a boy caring for his father's flock of sheep. Later on, he's spoken about by King Saul's servants, who call him a "brave man and a warrior" (1 Samuel 16:18). After this, Goliath challenges the Israelites to send a champion to fight him. David convinces King Saul to choose him as their fighter by citing his shepherding experiences: "When a lion or a bear came and carried off a sheep from the flock, I went after it, struck it and rescued the sheep from its mouth. When it turned on me, I seized it by its hair, struck it and killed it. Your servant has killed both the lion and the bear" (1 Samuel 17:34b-36a). Saul agrees, and David goes to fight Goliath, killing him by using his sling—with precision gained from years of practice protecting his flock from wild animals—to launch a stone into Goliath's forehead.

David's story shows us that shepherds were not meek, passive, or timid. David drew from firsthand experience when he wrote about God as our Shepherd in Psalm 23, depicting what life looks like when we belong to the Good Shepherd.

A good shepherd allows his sheep to rest in green pastures, leads them to calm water, stays with them as he leads them through dark valleys, and oils their heads to repel flies. Isaiah 40:11 tells us that not only are shepherds brave, protective warriors, but they're tender, compassionate lovers: "He tends his flock like a shepherd: He gathers the lambs in his arms and carries them close to his heart; he gently leads those that have young." When you are faithfully following the Lord in obedience, He will continually provide for you, comfort you, and give your weary soul rest. As you walk through this dark valley of betrayal, be assured His presence is with you. You are safe because you are His.

At the end of Psalm 23, David says, "...I will dwell in the house of the LORD forever" (verse 6b). Being in the household of God is a package deal! It includes an instant family of fellow believers. We have the entire flock of believers to help us keep our eyes on the Shepherd. Sheep have a natural instinct to stick together. An isolated sheep is an easy target for a mountain lion or coyote, so the last thing we want while we're in crisis is to be alone.

When a newborn lamb is separated from its mother, a shepherd will use the curved end of his staff to guide the baby back towards the mama ewe. If he were to touch the lamb with his hands, his human scent would get on the lamb, and it could cause the mama ewe to reject it. The shepherd knows what is best for both the lamb and the ewe, and he intervenes with his staff when necessary. Jesus' staff comforts us today. My Good Shepherd knew what was best for me. He hand-directed a flock of sheep to surround me when I was lonely and afraid.

The women who stayed close to me in my dark valley were my sister and a few other wise women of great faith. They seldom gave advice; these ladies simply reoriented me towards God. They were constantly reminding me to keep my eyes on Jesus, follow His guidance, and let Him tend to me. Having a group of women encouraging me with truth was such a great blessing. They sent Bible verses that would refresh my soul and would also speak truth in love (like when they reminded me that Will wasn't the enemy that wanted to destroy me, Satan was). We worshiped together via shared links on social media. Not all my texts to them were coherent; some were simply a "Please pray!" tapped out in the middle of the night or before a counseling session, but those women heard my heart and interceded on my behalf. We followed the Shepherd together, listening to Him as he called us by name.

God knows that we are totally incapable of staying on His path of righteousness solely using our own strength. Like sheep, we are prone to wander. Isaiah 53:6a says, "We all, like sheep, have gone astray, each of us has turned to our own way." Our brains love the path of least resistance. The panic that comes with betrayal might tempt us plug our ears and ignore God's voice. The paths of revenge, self-dependence, and unfaithfulness to God seem a whole lot easier than obedience.

We might move towards the toxic weeds of gossip or slander. Maybe we say things that provide momentary relief from rage but end up making us feel vulgar and ugly. One of my favorite "sheep," a mama ewe of sorts, talked sense into me one afternoon. I was expressing my "right" to be angry with Will. I justified the harmful words I had spoken by telling her he deserved them. She pointed out that as God's child, I did not have the "right" to sin just because I was angry. The righteous and appropriate response from a follower of Jesus would not be to let unwholesome talk come out of my mouth, but to utter only what is helpful for building others up according to their needs (Ephesians 4:29). While her admonition did not feel good or helpful at the time, her words of truth, spoken in love, directed my thoughts and words toward a more desirable path.

Other times we might head towards rocky cliffs, numbing the pain with alcohol or even trying to punish our husbands by having an affair ourselves. These actions create even more problems, compounding the effects of the original problem and putting our families at risk.

Thankfully, Jesus is our merciful and gracious Shepherd. He never leads us on a path towards sin, and His goodness and love pursues us relentlessly. He invites us, "Come to me, all you who are weary and burdened, and I will give you rest. Take my yoke upon you and learn from me, for I am gentle and humble in heart, and you will find rest for your souls. For my yoke is easy and my burden is light" (Matthew 11:28-30). When we run away, He gently calls us back. He might discipline us and place us over his shoulder and carry us a while, but this is done in His perfect love. There, on His shoulders, we're loved unconditionally. We learn we are safe with Him and can trust His leadership.

Jesus' invitation to follow Him wasn't just for His disciples. It's for you, too. He's inviting you to be in His flock. The book of Micah says, "Your king will lead you; the LORD himself will guide you" (Micah 2:13b NLT). When we willingly follow our Shepherd King's voice, yield to Him in obedience, and release our life into His protective hands, we receive the benefits and blessings of being His. We lack nothing and our burden is light. We will never lose our way. Who better to care for you, provide for you, and lead you, than the One who laid down His life for you? We walk the path of the one we're following. Whose voice are you listening to?

Prayer for Today

Lord, You are the Good Shepherd. I am thankful You always have the best in mind for me. Please continue to lead me with Your Word. Help me to trust Your way, even when it's difficult.

Questions to Ponder

1. How have you noticed the Lord encouraging you in your walk with Him? If His voice has been difficult to hear lately, tell Him. Let Him know you desire to hear and follow.

2. As your trust in the Lord grows, what new territory is He leading you into? What kind of sheep are you? Is He dragging you? Leading you? Breaking your legs? What might you need to surrender in order to follow?

3. Read John 10:1-18. List the spiritual blessings that come with being one of God's sheep. Take a moment to thank Him.

Chapter 15

Fitted and Ready

"For the word of God is alive and active. Sharper than
any double-edged sword, it penetrates even to dividing soul
and spirit, joints and marrow; it judges the thoughts
and attitudes of the heart."

Hebrews 4:12

When our oldest son was a baby, I joined a year-long Bible study that required six days' worth of active studying per week. At first, the commitment seemed overwhelming, but when I started studying, my hunger for the Word of God grew. By the time I had my second son, I had committed the first hour of every morning to the Lord. I would set my alarm for 5 a.m. because my boys woke up at 6 a.m. During Will's lengthy deployments, when everything was a little more difficult, 5 a.m. became the bright spot of my day. Waking up that early wasn't a burden.

In His presence, there was peace and calm. I was loved and not lonely. I entrusted all worries about the war and my husband's safety to the Lord. My tired mother's heart was encouraged, and as a single mom I gained wisdom in how to depend on Him. My kids knew this was my special time with God. If they woke up early, they stayed in bed until their Okay-to-Wake clock showed a happy face.

I cherished this time immersed in Scripture. Through the years, God was developing my love for Him and the Bible. He was arming me with His Word. The strength I developed during this time enabled me to withstand the suffering I would later face.

Proper armor is necessary if we're going to survive life's disappointments, tragedies, and unexpected losses. Paul knew what it was like to battle an unseen Enemy. In a letter he wrote two thousand years ago to the Ephesian church, he instructed the congregants on how to arm themselves against attacks:

> *Finally, be strong in the Lord and in his mighty power. Put on the full armor of God, so that you can take your stand against the devil's schemes. For our struggle is not against flesh and blood, but against the rulers, against the authorities, against the powers of this dark world and against the spiritual forces of evil in the heavenly realms. Therefore put on the full armor of God, so that when the day of evil comes, you may be able to stand your ground, and after you have done everything, to stand. Stand firm then, with the belt of truth buckled around your waist, with the breastplate of righteousness in place, and with your feet fitted with the readiness that comes from the gospel of peace. In addition to all this, take up the shield of faith, with which you can extinguish all the flaming arrows of the evil one. Take the helmet of salvation and the sword of the Spirit, which is the word of God.* (Ephesians 6:10-17)

Did you notice the sword is the only weapon of offense listed? The breastplate, shield, and helmet are necessary for preservation of life, but the Word of God is the only thing listed we can use against the Enemy.

When the Holy Spirit led Jesus into the wilderness after His baptism, Luke tells us He was tempted by the devil for forty days (Luke 4:1-2)! He had been fasting during this time and was hungry. I know some people don't think clearly when they're "hangry." They ask not to be held accountable for things they say when it's twenty minutes past their regular lunchtime, and they haven't eaten. Thankfully, Jesus set a better example. In response to Satan's temptations, Jesus fought him by quoting Scripture, enabling Jesus to prevail against the attacks.

We need to learn and retain God's Word. Jesus demonstrated how we can use Scripture to examine the Enemy's deception and identify his lies for what they are. Anything that contradicts God's Word is not true! We have to be careful and discerning, especially if we've been living in "crisis-mode." First Peter 5:8 warns us: "Be alert and of sober mind. Your enemy the devil prowls around like a roaring lion looking for someone to devour." A woman who appears abandoned, rejected, and in despair is the perfect target for Satan to sink his claws into. But take heart! You are not defenseless. God has prepared you with the armor you need. He has given you the greatest treasure in the world: the Sword of the Spirit, which is the Word of God.

Hebrews 4:12 describes this treasure: "For the word of God is alive and active. Sharper than any double-edged sword, it penetrates even to dividing soul and spirit, joints and marrow; it judges the thoughts and attitudes of the heart." I like the detail of the type of sword because a single-edged sword lacerates, while a double-edged sword pierces. If I'm battling an enemy, give me a double-edged sword, please!

Maybe you don't feel equipped to fight the battle ahead, but there's good news. You don't have to fight alone or unequipped! The Sword of the Spirit, the Word of God, is accessible to us all. Never once have I regretted waking up at 5 a.m. to read His words in Scripture. There are so many benefits to taking His words to heart. They bring wisdom and discernment. They help us fight against the Enemy's temptations and lies. They convict us of the sin in our lives and encourage us with the limitless grace and love of God. The Word shapes us to live our lives in a way that honors God.

When Will wasn't deployed, it was trickier to find time to myself for my Bible study. He wasn't exactly open to me putting an Okay-to-Wake clock on his nightstand. After I learned of his infidelity, there were mornings when waking up at 5 a.m. seemed downright impossible. It was much more tempting to pull the blankets over my head and claim it was not Okay-to-Wake for me, either.

However, it's when we don't feel like arming ourselves with the Word of God that we need it even more. Remember the type of woman Satan likes to prey on? The more I refrained from God's Word, the less prepared I was for when Satan inevitably attacked. God calls us to have our armor on, properly fitted, for *when* (not IF) that day comes. It's not wise to throw our armor to the side, then hastily try to put it on when the Enemy springs from a dark corner. Don't leave yourself open and vulnerable to a surprise attack! After a betrayal, spending time in the Word is more important than ever.

Your mind is not an empty vessel. If it's not being filled up with the Word of God, the world and its ungodly advice will fill it. Maybe you've already heard some of the world's advice for how to respond to your husband's betrayal: "Smear him on social media; he deserves it." "I'll help you slash his tires." "Don't let him see the kids. That'll teach him."

When we turn our itching ears away from truth, we're losing ground. There's a possibility you'll be lured into overindulging in food, wine, gossip, social media, or binge-watching movies, instead of digging into the Bible for help. Maybe there's a temptation to isolate in bed under a load of self-pity, or sit with company who will smear your husband with you. We can't let Satan win in these ways. It's destructive to us, to others, and to our relationship with God.

As I've witnessed with my husband, soldiers are prepared. They know their enemy, their weapons, their equipment, their hand signals, and their mission. In their training, they are repeatedly put into stressful, complex scenarios to simulate combat. As a result, they form neural synapses that enable them to respond to an attack effectively without having to stop to think about their response first. When it's time to go to battle, they take what they have learned and put all their effort into completing their goal. They rely on their training and can make effective split-second decisions when lives are at stake.

We can build our own neural synapses for effectively fighting the Enemy, just like Jesus did in the desert. We can even take the handbook into battle with us. Because of amazing advances in technology, we can have the Word of God at our fingertips, in a matter of seconds, in a multitude of languages and translations. We can continually train, even on the battlefield. The more familiar we are with the Bible, the easier it will be to recall the exact passages we need in the moment of attack. The more we are in the Word, the better able we are to identify the wiles of the Enemy. Knowledge is power when it is knowledge of the Word of God, life of Jesus, and indwelling of the Holy Spirit, all of which help us know how wily and evil the Enemy is.

In 2 Timothy 3:16-17, Paul gives a final charge to his dear friend Timothy. At the time, the Christian church was experiencing severe persecution under Roman Emperor Nero. Paul admonished Timothy to remember and hold fast to the truth he had learned in Scripture. Paul writes, "All Scripture is God-breathed and is useful for teaching, rebuking, correcting and training in righteousness, so that the servant of God may be thoroughly equipped for every good work." This is my charge to you too, my sister in Christ. We're in this fight together. Let's be prepared and equipped for every good work by holding God's Word, the Sword of the Spirit, close to our hearts. It's all we need.

Take that, Satan.

Prayer for Today

Your word is a lamp for my feet,

a light on my path.

I have taken an oath and confirmed it,

that I will follow your righteous laws.

I have suffered much;

preserve my life, LORD, according to your word.

Accept, LORD, the willing praise of my mouth,

and teach me your laws.

Though I constantly take my life in my hands,

I will not forget your law.

The wicked have set a snare for me,

but I have not strayed from your precepts.

Your statutes are my heritage forever;

they are the joy of my heart.

My heart is set on keeping your decrees

to the very end. (Psalm 119:105-112)

Questions to Ponder

1. How does the exhortation in 1 Peter 5:8 affect you? What spiritual disciplines can you put into place to protect yourself from being deceived by the Enemy? How can you get dressed in the full armor of God on a daily basis?

2. At what times do you find yourself most grateful for God's Word? How will you choose to thank Him for providing you with this weapon of offense?

3. Jesus is our perfect example of how to respond to the Enemy. What is one verse that you can commit to memory to help you when you feel tempted or attacked? Consider these as a start: 1 Timothy 6:11; James 4:7; Philippians 4:13, and 1 Peter 5:8-11.

Chapter 16

Beyond the Fairy Tale

"Finally, brothers and sisters, whatever is true, whatever is noble, whatever is right, whatever is pure, whatever is lovely, whatever is admirable—if anything is excellent or praiseworthy—think about such things."

Philippians 4:8

A voicemail from my husband: "Hey Babe, would you mind calling the plumber today and having him unclog the drain upstairs? I'd rather not have to deal with the sink tonight after work. I've had such a busy week. I just want to spend the evening with you. I've really missed you and the kids. Maybe a game night or a movie? Whatever you want, I know you're feeling exhausted from yesterday, too. Oh, I forgot to tell you, I filled your van up with gas last night. I hope that helps you get to your meeting a little earlier. Love you, Beautiful."

Maybe by the time you got to "call the plumber," you realized this was a made-up voicemail from my imaginary ideal husband—a man who serves me with acts of kindness; would rather spend time with his family than under a faucet; acknowledges my exhaustion; shows gratitude, and prays for me daily. Wow, what a guy! This make-believe voice message is an example of how my mind can wander, making up stories about a perfect husband. I bet you've done it, too.

119

I got married at nineteen. My general expectations about marriage were unreasonable, and I had no idea what being married to a military man would be like. My dad had served in the Army, but I was too young to remember that. I didn't grow up in a military town or know anyone else who had served.

During Will's first deployment while we were still dating, we wrote lots of letters back and forth in which we imagined our future together. We'd have a big ranch home in the country, full of kids. We'd watch Saturday night sunsets in our rocking chairs from our wraparound porch. Our dog would be perfectly trained. We'd work at the same small community hospital together. We even joked we'd have a babysitter on-call for weekend date nights.

Obviously, like most other couples, our married life has looked much different than what we pictured. Instead of all the dreams we'd penned to each other while we dated, our marriage has been birthdays and holidays with Will online, sitting by myself in church, and us becoming good friends with other military families who eventually moved away. We've dealt with the traumatic effects of war, and the death of friends. We've both experienced loneliness and exhaustion. At times, we've both buried feelings of bitterness and resentment. We've also made countless wonderful memories.

After Will confessed to his affairs, it became increasingly difficult to conjure those in my mind. I was frustrated I never got the idealized ending. I often found myself wondering why we got married in the first place.

My mind would take me to a different life, married to a different man. Sometimes it happened at church when the couple in front of me was worshiping with their arms around each other's waists, sometimes when I saw a husband open the car door for his wife. Sometimes the thoughts came when I watched a movie that was a fairy tale love story. I longed for a relationship like that. If a man like that was out there, I wanted to find him.

I didn't consider how things aren't always what they seemed. Maybe that cuddly couple in church was comforting each other over the loss of a loved one. Maybe the husband opening the door for his wife was doing so because she had debilitating arthritis. The movie was fictional.

This started to lead me down the wrong path. As I continued in this fantasy world of what life would have been like if I had just married the perfect man, I became more and more dissatisfied. That's how the Enemy works. He doesn't pull us kicking and screaming down the wayward path; he just convinces us to take the next small step, think the next small thought, imagine the next small detail. When we're willing to do that, our attitudes become more and more discontent. We give the Devil a foothold, and our thought patterns become cluttered with lies and temptation.

When we let our imaginations run wild with unrealistic expectations, unhealthy thoughts, and "what ifs," we're leaving our minds vulnerable to the Enemy. We risk stepping into temptation, crossing boundaries that are contrary to our morals, and taking risks that are against our better judgment. It's dangerous territory. It could lead us to seek revenge by having an affair ourselves. We are not immune to temptation. Our minds are a battlefield, and we need to protect them with the wisdom of God.

We see this progression of temptation when we read Proverbs chapter 7. There, we find a young, senseless man inching towards sin one disobedient step at a time. We meet him walking down the street near the house of an adulteress. Soon, he's heading towards her home as dusk falls. Red flag! It's time to go home, but instead of noticing the darkness and listening to wisdom, he walks to her door.

The adulteress is dressed like a prostitute when she comes out to meet him—another red flag. She grabs him and kisses him. She tells him how glad she is to see him and that she's been looking for him. Lies. She would have taken any fool who chose to walk in her direction.

She's probably worn those harlot clothes for many others. Did he really think that he was "the one" that she had been waiting for? Red flag!

I can't help but want to protect this guy from his own downfall. *Run away, dude. She's lying to you!* Instead, he stays and continues to listen. She tells him her husband is on a long trip and won't be home for some time. WARNING, WARNING! Double red flag! If nothing else has made him want to turn away, this should have! If he gets caught by her husband, he's toast! One more step, and he's dead:

> *With persuasive words she led him astray;*
> *she seduced him with her smooth talk.*
> *All at once, he followed her*
> *like an ox going to slaughter,*
> *like a deer stepping into a noose*
> *till an arrow pierces his liver,*
> *like a bird darting into a snare,*
> *little knowing it would cost him his life.* (Proverbs 7:21-23)

Do you see how this man was led straight to death, one step at a time? There were so many opportunities to save himself, so many chances to run. Unfortunately, in our thought life, we do this, too.

My heart's desire is to have my mind filled with godly wisdom instead of discontentment and complaints. I want to know how to stand against temptation instead of stepping towards it. I want to make God-honoring decisions, using careful judgment and discernment.

This was also my heart's desire when my life was turned upside down, but images of the physical acts of my husband's infidelity started to frequently invade my mind once he confessed. These thoughts were different from my previous ones comparing my relationship to others and daydreaming about my ideal husband. I didn't invite these thoughts in, or deliberately choose to meditate on them, they just showed up unannounced (usually at the most inconvenient times).

It felt like my mind was turning against me. Images of my husband with faceless women bombarded my thoughts while I was driving, cleaning, and most often, when I was lying awake in bed late at night. They felt dirty—something I knew I shouldn't be thinking about. Once they started, they would continue into all hours of the night. They would lead me to tears, anger, and more anxiety. I knew the thoughts were constantly tormenting me, but I couldn't get a handle on them. I wanted to have some kind of control over my thought life again. I knew God promised to: "Keep in perfect peace those whose minds are steadfast, because they trust in [Him]" (Isaiah 26:3). I wanted that peace, but how could I train my mind to remain steadfast?

Thankfully, God, in His loving mercy and compassion, didn't condemn me or shame me for my thoughts. Instead, He taught me what to do with them. Our omniscient God is the God of Wisdom. James 1:5 tells us that if we ask God for the wisdom we lack, He will give generously.

I asked God for His wisdom and guidance, and He provided, again and again. He directed me to Philippians 4:8: "Finally, brothers and sisters, whatever is true, whatever is noble, whatever is right, whatever is pure, whatever is lovely, whatever is admirable—if anything is excellent or praiseworthy—think about such things."

As I meditated on this verse, I remembered how my sister had taught her eight-year-old son to use it to take back control of his thoughts. He had been having bad dreams, and she had encouraged him to memorize this verse. He would wake up in distress, then wake her up. She would ask him to recite the verse, then ask, "What is something that is true?"

"My parents love me," he'd answer.

"Then think about that. What is something that is noble?"

"A king who does right for his people."

"Then think about that."

I thought to myself, *if an eight-year-old child can practically apply God's Word to calm himself enough to go back to sleep, then I can, too.*

123

When the reel of affairs started playing, and I began to feel rejected and unloved, I'd ask myself, *What is true?*

The answer was that God's Word says I am a daughter of the King (1 John 3:1). I am chosen and I am loved.

When I was angry that my family was at risk of being broken apart by sin, I asked myself, *What is noble?*

The answer was that He loves me so much that He laid His wrath on His own son, punishing Him instead of me (1 Thessalonians 1:10). He fights for me, has rescued me, and is worthy of my gratitude forever (2 Samuel 22:4).

When I started to imagine text messages or conversations Will exchanged with other women, I would stop myself by asking, *What is right?* The Word of God says that God is perfect in all of His ways (Psalm 18:30). He is righteous and just (Psalm 11:7).

When I inadvertently imagined Will's past actions of infidelity and felt panicked and insecure, I'd immediately ask, *What is pure?* The Bible teaches that Jesus is pure (1 John 3:3). The spotless Lamb of God (John 1:29) is holy, blameless, pure, set apart from sinners, exalted above the heavens (Hebrews 7:26). He was the perfect sacrifice required for my sin (Hebrews 9:14).

Sometimes I would compare my aging mom body to what I imagined a sexy porn actress' body would look like. Remembering my body was created by God and was a temple of the Holy Spirit, I would ask myself, *What is lovely?* The answer was my relationship with Jesus. It's a relationship that will extend into Heaven, where I'll spend eternity in the presence of Love Himself (John 3:16).

At first, my thoughts felt as if they were bouncing around like the ball in a pinball game. With time and practice, using the tools found in His Word, I was able to take back control of my thoughts. God created our minds and knows how powerful they are. He knows that we are prone to discontentment, comparison, and deception by the Enemy. He knows when you've been criticized by your husband and gossiped about or judged by others in regards to your relationship with your husband. He knows when others have played mind-games with you and gaslighted you so much that you second-guess yourself at every turn now.

As followers of Christ, we are called to put off our old self and be made new in the attitude of our minds (Ephesians 4:23). This renewing will cause transformation in every area of our lives, bolstering our faith and encouraging obedience to Him.

I am so thankful God instructed Paul to write down how to handle our thoughts with wisdom, to reject lies, and to focus our minds on Jesus. When we think about what is true, noble, right, pure, lovely, and admirable, we walk—one step at a time—towards Jesus.

Wisdom is not just acts of reading and listening to God's Word. It's discerning God's voice from the Enemy's lies and putting God's Word into practice (James 1:22). It's dwelling on the next true thought, concentrating on the next right step, and fixing our eyes on the One who is worthy of our praise. Paul finishes his instructions for reclaiming our thoughts with a call to obedience and a promise that we can cling to: "Whatever you have learned or received or heard from me, or seen in me—put it into practice. And the God of peace will be with you" (Philippians 4:9).

Prayer For Today

Lord, thank You for being the God of Peace. When ungodly thoughts enter my mind, I look to You for help. Please continue to renew my mind with Your wisdom. I want my thoughts to continually honor You.

Questions to Ponder

1. Make your own list. What is true? Noble? Right? Pure? Lovely? Admirable? Excellent? Praiseworthy? Think about these things.

2. Read Matthew 22:37. How can you love the Lord your God with all of your mind today? How will you invite Jesus close when ugly thoughts invade your mind?

3. In what place or time of day are you most tempted to fix your eyes on the problem, instead of on Jesus? What verses can you call to mind when that happens?

Chapter 17

Forgiving the Unforgivable

*"When I am afraid, I put my trust in you. In God,
whose word I praise—in God I trust and am not afraid.
What can mere mortals do to me?"*

Psalm 56:3-4

During our recovery, Will attended a peer-based recovery program for men in the military and law enforcement. It was designed to help them identify and process the challenges their fields entailed, including post-traumatic stress, and to move forward into lives of biblical manhood.

Will had heard great things about this program for years. He'd even referred friends and coworkers to it, though he had never attended himself. God's timing was perfect though, and Will was able to go when he needed it most—four months after D-Day. While the program was not specifically designed for those working through infidelity in marriage, I knew it had potential for lasting impact in our relationship.

The four months prior to his first day in the program hadn't been spent idly. Will and I had been in counseling (both individual and couples counseling) and completed the requisite "homework" from our therapists. We'd met regularly with our pastor, joined groups specifically designed for our kinds of hurts, and committed to each other to do whatever it would take to save our marriage. The morning he left to attend the retreat, I was confident he would wholeheartedly participate in it.

He came home from the program with a renewed desire to be obedient to God. These brothers in Christ encouraged him to grow into the man, husband, and father God designed him to be. He saw it was necessary to change how he had been living, and told me the practical ways he intended to do it. It wasn't like he came home as Husband 2.0, but I saw how his heart was starting to unite with the heart of God.

Later, the program staff held a week-long event for the wives of group members. Will asked me to consider going.

As I filled out the online application for the event, I secretly hoped I would be denied a spot. I was reluctant to go, because it would mean an eight-hour drive each way, plus being away from my home and family. I would also have to meet and converse with upwards of thirty strangers, something I found overwhelming as a shy introvert. I loved sharing transparently with a small group of two or three trusted friends, but in a large group setting, I usually preferred listening. I knew the event had the potential to spark change, healing, and growth in me, but also knew I would be very uncomfortable in the process. I pressed "submit," still feeling awkward and unconvinced about it, like a preteen on the first day of junior high.

I was accepted into the program. A short time later, I packed my bags, left my family, and drove the eight hours there. Once the event started, I quickly realized the other wives attending had entered into the process wholeheartedly. They wanted healing, to be relieved from the burdens they carried. They wanted whatever God had for them that week.

On the first night, I met a woman I'll call Destiny. I instantly liked her. She was real and didn't hide behind a polite smile and small talk. She worked full-time as a law enforcement officer and shared with me about the struggles of her job. She had lost coworkers and friends in shootings, and she herself had almost died on multiple occasions. As a result of these stresses and hardships, she wrestled with anxiety. She had come to this gathering to find peace and rest for her soul and wanted to go deeper in her relationship with the Lord.

The next morning, clad in the typical California retreat attire of flip flops and hoodies, Destiny and I met the other women at the firepit. As we drank coffee, the others began to share about why they were there. One woman said she'd just had a miscarriage and that had the baby lived, it would have been her and her husband's first child. Another woman opened up about her struggles with depression and drug use. I was content to just be a listener, and my heart mourned with each woman as she shared the pains held deepest in her heart.

As I listened to the women around me, I also decided I didn't want to be there at all. Something about the fact that they were quickly moving to vulnerability made me realize that it would soon be my turn. Sure enough, when there was a lull in the conversation, someone said, "You haven't shared yet, Robin. Why are you here?"

I didn't want to share with people I'd just met that my husband had come home from a deployment to tell me he didn't think he loved me anymore; that it felt as if I'd been living a lie for the past ten years; that our marriage had been destroyed by betrayal. Then again, I realized the women around me also wished their stories were not theirs to tell.

Even after listening to their courageous disclosures, I still feared being open to critique and judgment if I shared. *What if they doubted my abilities as a wife? What if they wondered what I had done to cause my husband to stray? Would they think I had been self-absorbed and that was why I hadn't even noticed my husband was cheating? Maybe they'd even judge my lack of discernment for staying in the marriage.* I didn't want the unsolicited feedback of, "You know, once a cheater, always a cheater." And, "There's no way I could ever stay with a man who…" I felt the pressure building and my tears coming, but the Lord gave me courage. I began to share.

The Lord didn't leave me alone in that circle. Those fears of being judged or criticized were dashed in an instant. Every woman there responded with the heart of God, overflowing with compassion, sympathy, and love. I shared transparently, and God ended up using it for His glory.

On the last morning, each participant was asked to share how God had worked in her life that week. Destiny bravely went first. My tough cop friend hadn't cried the entire week, but suddenly, she began to weep before her words even came out. She kept eye contact with me and shared how she used to be "the other woman." Before she was married to her husband, she had knowingly had sex with married men. It was a twisted way in which she tried to find value and worth. She had never told anyone this before and had never repented of it. Knowing what I had been through, she said to me, "I know you probably hate me, Robin, but I am so, so, so sorry."

"I don't hate you. You are forgiven," I said to my own surprise.

I hadn't even fully thought through my response before I had said it. It had come out naturally. Hearing the hurt in her voice made my heart hurt. She needed to know immediately that the Lord had already forgiven her. It wasn't necessary for her to hold onto that burden on my account. Afterwards, I began to feel the Holy Spirit gently guiding me to forgive the women whose lives and stories were now inextricably woven into my own life and marriage.

Sometimes, I wished the women who had been involved with my husband would be so burdened with guilt that they would need to seek my forgiveness. I wondered what I would say in reply if they approached me with an apology, but they never did. I will likely never receive an apology from them.

Maybe, in your situation, the same woman is repeating the offense over and over again with no remorse. Maybe it's the way she earns a living. She may choose to continue doing so and never realize the agony of being on the other side. Maybe it's the opposite. The woman doesn't even realize she has done anything wrong because she didn't know your husband was married.

I don't know any of the other women that were involved with my husband, but maybe you knew your offenders, and that's gut-wrenching. Maybe it was your best friend or a neighbor who you were just beginning to confide in. I hate that this has happened to you.

I want to tell you something else that surprised me: seeing a repentant adulteress' anguish, pain, and sorrow wasn't as satisfying as I imagined it would be. Sin is ugly. It can cause cruel consequences for both the perpetrator and the victim.

Destiny hadn't come to the program to seek forgiveness or to work through the shame associated with her actions. It wasn't even on her radar. She had been focused on working through her grief and anxiety surrounding her career, but the Lord had other plans that week. He longed to free her from the pain she hadn't even realized she'd been carrying for years. He used my story to gently bring her to sorrow over her sin, guide her to repentance, and receive forgiveness.

I didn't go to the program with the intention of forgiving the "other women." It felt too soon. It wasn't on my radar, but the Lord had other plans that week for me, too. He surprised me with the gift of Destiny's apology and gave me the courage to start forgiving. This was the most impactful memory I have of that week, and if it was the only reason God gave me the courage to attend, it was entirely worth it.

I understand fully that the thought of forgiving the other woman, especially when she's not even sorry, might feel like you're allowing her to get away with murder. Certainly, your marriage as you knew it has been murdered. At the same time, we absolutely cannot allow the absence of an apology to justify holding onto bitterness and unforgiveness. I am not implying you should approach the woman or women who hurt you, but in the stillness of your heart, talk to God about it. He knows how difficult this is. He forgave the very people who were nailing His hands to the cross and watching Him suffocate. He will meet you where you're at. As you spend time with Him, in His Word and in prayer, ask Him for the courage to do what He's asked you to do. If it takes some time, that's okay! It may take less time than you expect. It may take more.

If someone would have told me on D-Day that I would reach this point in my healing process so rapidly, I probably would have thrown a latté at her. It's never too soon, or too late, to turn away from our anger and towards God. As a good friend always says, "It's a process." The important part isn't how quickly you get to this point, it's that you listen to the prompting of the Holy Spirit as He leads you. He's not going to abandon you in the process. He always equips His daughters with the things they need to be obedient. He will supply you with the courage and strength to forgive.

Prayer for Today

Lord, thank You that in Your sovereignty, You create learning experiences and opportunities for me to grow. Sometimes obedience is difficult and uncomfortable. I want to surrender my whole heart to You. Please give me the courage I need to do what You say. Help me to forgive.

Questions to Ponder

1. Take some time to talk to God about how difficult and far-reaching forgiveness feels. Ask Him to help you open your heart to the idea of forgiveness.

2. In what ways does knowing the Lord is your Helper give you confidence to obey, even when it's difficult?

3. Read Joshua 1:9. How does this verse encourage you? How does the promise of God's constant presence bring you peace?

Chapter 18

His Way is Perfect

"As for God, his way is perfect…"

2 Samuel 22:31a

Will's sin invaded my marriage, my life, and my home. When I found out, I wanted vengeance; he needed to pay severely for what he'd done to me and our family. Sixteen years of marriage had been shredded to pieces. No consequence would ever be enough for the havoc he'd caused. These thoughts of retribution swamped my mind, and I wanted Will stuck in a vice grip of shame. I asked God to avenge me, to make Will pay for what he had done.

I'm sure you've been there, too. As humans, we intuitively know the difference between right and wrong, and we have a strong desire to see wrongdoing punished. We also tend to judge others more severely when their sin impacts us.

Habakkuk, a prophet from the land of Judah, experienced some of the same emotions that we've felt. Habakkuk lived in a time where the people of Judah were acting in direct defiance of the Lord, engaging in everything from idol worship to child sacrifices to public orgies. Habakkuk was surrounded by violence, evil, and wickedness. He was heartbroken that the people who had seen and experienced God's marvelous works and provision were now abandoning Him.

Furthermore, Habakkuk felt desperate and confused because it seemed like God was tolerating their behavior.

At the beginning of the story, Habakkuk says, "How long, LORD, must I call for help, but you do not listen? ...Why do you make me look at injustice? Why do you tolerate wrongdoing?" (Habakkuk 1:2-3a). Habakkuk took his concerns and confusion straight to God. We can learn from his bold approach. God knows we long for the wrongs committed against us to be righted. He welcomes our questions and concerns when we're struggling to understand.

God replied to Habakkuk's complaint by telling Habakkuk He wasn't excusing the horrendous behavior or condoning it. He just hadn't responded yet. He let Habakkuk in on His plan: God said that, in His time, He would raise up the ruthless Babylonians to punish Judah. They would invade Judah, capture the people, and lead them to another land with hooks in their mouths. God's answer shocked Habakkuk, and his confusion only intensified as they kept talking.

Habakkuk knew about the Babylonians and their evil. He complained a second time: "Why then do you tolerate the treacherous? Why are you silent while the wicked swallow up those more righteous than themselves?" (1:13b). He thought Judah's consequences were going to be too severe. Why would God punish Judah with a nation even more wicked than they were? God confirmed that in time, Babylonia would also experience His wrath.

This conversation between God and Habakkuk goes back and forth for three chapters with Habakkuk complaining and God giving him confusing answers. Habakkuk starts to shift his attitude and begins trusting and praising God. Habakkuk prays, "LORD, I have heard of your fame; I stand in awe of your deeds, LORD. Repeat them in our day, in our time make them known; in wrath, remember mercy" (3:2). He praises God for His holiness, describes His glory and splendor, and chooses to rejoice in the LORD God, his Savior.

We can see Habakkuk's change of heart as we read the last chapter. He says with his lips quivering and heart pounding, "I will wait patiently for the day of calamity" (3:16). Habakkuk was now confidently trusting God with the outcome of His people. In the end, he believed God's plans were best.

God's desire is that we live in an unhindered relationship with Him. However, God is perfect love, and He can't tolerate sin. Every sin is offensive to Him and cannot go unpunished. Judah's sin needed to be dealt with, just like our sin does. Since the beginning of time, God knew we were incapable of a sinless life, so He arranged a plan for us. The plan was to send His perfect Son, Jesus Christ, to earth to pay the price that our sin deserved. Jesus lived a sinless life and became the necessary sacrifice to satisfy our debt. It is only because of this gift of grace that we can have a relationship with God. When we repent from our sin, we are forgiven for every wrong—past, present, and future. We can never out-sin God's grace.

Perhaps God is calling your husband to Himself, but your husband isn't responding in repentance. Maybe you've prayed and prayed that your husband would see the error in his ways, but he's on the same destructive path he's been on for years. I understand the anger that comes from thinking your husband is "getting off the hook" or "getting away with" his behavior. Maybe he's carrying on in his pornography addiction or he's wasting your family income on prostitutes. Maybe he's crossing every single boundary the two of you decided on, and it seems like God should be intervening on your behalf.

Why isn't God setting your husband straight, fixing the situation, or repaying him for the hurt he's caused? The injustice of it all seems like too much to bear. The comfort comes in knowing that when our husbands have done us wrong, we can entrust them and the entire situation into God's hands. The way God handles our situations with our husbands will be consistent with His character. His way is perfect.

Even though God forgives us of sin, we still must reckon with its consequences. I knew the side-effects of what Will had done would impact our family for years to come. Whether or not Will and I stayed married, I would have to suffer under the fallout, and that felt unfair. Why should I have to deal with the ramifications of choices I had no part in?

What if I had a sexually transmitted infection that had been dormant in my body for years? How would I respond if a child my husband fathered showed up on our doorstep someday? If that child surfaced, how would that impact our reputation, especially in our Christian community? If we chose divorce, my life would be drastically different, as I would become a full-time single mother. Having never experienced the sting of betrayal before, I didn't know what the consequences would look like, but I was sure of their arrival.

The ripple effect impacted almost every area of our lives. Healing and recovery is an uphill battle that requires time, patience, vulnerability, resilience, and energy. The money I spent on counseling sessions, digital filters, and accountability apps I would have rather used on family vacations. I also spent brainpower on scheduling the sessions and juggling childcare. Going to our support groups meant missing family dinners twice a week, plus we had to allot additional time to complete their requisite homework. My trust was not given freely; it had to be earned by responsible behavior repeated over time. Implementing boundaries, when done properly, felt like I was punishing myself. I would rather have avoided the uncomfortable conversations Will and I had to have.

How long did it take for Habakkuk to get to the point of surrendering the outcome of other people's lives into God's hands? I don't know, but I bet it took me longer to get to the same point. I wouldn't have admitted it openly, but during this time, I often thought I knew better than God about how things should go. I was constantly reminded, though, through God's Word and wise counsel, that His way was far better than any plan I came up with myself. He is just and fair, no matter what I think would be best. God's purpose in discipline is always to restore His people to Himself. That's why when consequences are part of the plotline, we don't have to worry!

In God's perfect way, He used the things I initially perceived as negative to express His fatherly love to both my husband and myself. The counseling appointments improved our communication and helped us figure out healthier ways to respond to one other. The digital filters and accountability apps worked well and helped to build trust over time. Our support groups encouraged us to keep our eyes fixed on God, pray for each other, serve each other well, and dig into the Word individually and as a couple. The boundaries we put in place made our relationship stronger. The truth is God had a perfect way of dealing with the impact the betrayal caused.

Perhaps you've been questioning God as to why you're the one suffering the consequences when your husband's the one who did wrong. Are you begging Him to take away this hurt you didn't instigate but now is a constant part of your life? It probably doesn't seem fair that you've been caught up in the backwash of your husband's sin. Are you working two jobs now because you can no longer count on your husband's income? Did you have to leave your church because the woman he was with sits in the row in front of you? Maybe you struggle with anxiety or depression now. As I write these words, I'm imagining how God will reveal Himself to you as your Provider and Comforter in all of your new changes and challenges. I'm confident that because He is good, you will not feel this pain forever.

God's ways are higher than our ways, and His thoughts are higher than our thoughts (Isaiah 55:9). God knows we can't understand all of the parts of this unwanted chapter in our lives. He didn't want sin to enter the story either. He expects that, like Habakkuk, we have concerns and confusion. We don't need to fear bringing our doubts and questions to Him. He welcomes them!

We can approach Him with awe and reverence for who He is. He may not give us the answers to every question—and with our limited understanding, we might perceive His conclusion as unfair—but wait on Him. As you wait, trust He is always fair and always right. He will deal with your situation in perfect love. The resolution of your story is in the Lord's hands, and He writes the best ones!

Prayer for Today

Lord, You wanted a relationship with me before time existed, and You made a way for it to happen. You know the outcome from the beginning. I trust You with the outcome of my marriage, how You choose to deal with my husband, the consequences of the betrayal, and how You're writing the rest of my story. Your plan is always the best plan. Your way is always perfect.

Questions to Ponder

1. What concerns, doubts, complaints, or questions have you been hesitant to bring to God? God wants to hear from you! Write out a prayer to Him and wait to see how He answers.

2. At the end of Habakkuk's book, he was confident that God's plans were the best plans. How does it help to know that God has always been, and always will be, sovereign?

3. What comfort does it bring you to know the outcome of your story is in the hands of the Sovereign One? What is your response to Him as you see glimpses of His perfect plan unfolding?

Chapter 19

A Case of Mistaken Identity

"For your Maker is your husband—
the L<small>ORD</small> *Almighty is His name..."*

Isaiah 54:5a

This past year, during one of my Bible studies, we dove deep into the book of Hosea. Because I grew up in a Christian home and regularly attended church throughout my life, I already had a basic knowledge of the prophet Hosea's story. God tells Hosea to marry Gomer, a woman known for her promiscuous reputation. Gomer cheats on Hosea, but God tells Hosea to take her back as his wife. God used Hosea's experience to prophesy His warning and His faithfulness to the wayward people of Israel.

I knew this book would be difficult to study, and I secretly started to dread it. I imagined the scabs on my healing heart might get irritated, or worse, ripped off completely. I contemplated skipping the homework portion entirely and scheduling something else during our group's meeting time that week. Lots of things could come up that might require my attention, like maybe my dog would need to go to the groomer's (the imaginary dog the kids had been begging to own for years). Wait, did I feel a tickle in my throat? One can never be too

139

cautious when it comes to health. Our group was pretty big. If I skipped out, they might not even notice I was missing.

As I wrestled with what to do, the Holy Spirit revealed that rather than trying to get out of it, I needed to read this book. Still, it was difficult for me to begin studying it. I knew God would reveal relevant, healing wisdom through Hosea, but the process of discovery probably wouldn't feel good. The Bible says, "All Scripture is God-breathed and is useful for teaching, rebuking, correcting and training in righteousness, so that the servant of God may be thoroughly equipped for every good work" (2 Timothy 3:16-17). I focused on these verses to assure myself, and remembered the Holy Spirit would be right there as I read, accompanying and guiding me.

Once I started reading Hosea, I was shocked. Some verses were difficult to read because of their explicit details. The King James version used the word "whore" unapologetically and frequently. As a spouse who knows what it's like to be forsaken, I identified with Hosea. Righteous anger toward Gomer rose out of me.

I imagined the grief and sorrow that Hosea must have been experiencing as his wife ran away from him and towards other lovers. I thought about the injustice Hosea must have felt as she credited her other lovers with providing her food, water, and clothing, when he was the one actually providing these things for her. He must have been indignant when Gomer became pregnant with other men's children. I pictured the tears of confusion streaming down his face as the Lord told him, "Go, show your love to your wife again, though she is loved by another man and is an adulteress" (Hosea 3:1a).

I paused before getting too far into the book, and whispered a prayer: "Lord, show me what you intend for me to learn here."

As I read on, I slowly began to understand that I was relating myself to the wrong character in the story. As someone who had been betrayed by a spouse, I had been reading from Hosea's perspective.

Because of my history, I had unconsciously chosen to misinterpret the story. I wasn't Hosea; God was.

God called Hosea to write this book as a metaphor of God's unfailing, covenant love for the Israelites, despite their worshiping of other gods. The marriage of Hosea and Gomer paralleled the relationship between God and His people. This most intimate type of betrayal was used to show how God grieved when His children walked away from Him. God was a faithful, committed husband who loved Israel with an everlasting love and provided everything she needed. Israel, on the other hand, continuously abandoned the Lord and rejected His ways while polluting herself with sin.

Even though I wanted to be the one doing the forgiving and calling back, it was only because God had called me back that I could offer forgiveness. I was reminded, "There is no one righteous, not even one" (Romans 3:10), and "For all have sinned and fall short of the glory of God" (verse 23). My forgiveness and righteousness before God comes through the sacrifice of Jesus' blood. We don't deserve this, but God is full of grace and love. He sanctifies us freely.

In the Old Testament, God frequently speaks of Israel as His bride. He chose Israel, out of all the other nations, to be His special possession. The stories of Abraham, Isaac, and Jacob were sovereignly pieced together, despite countless interruptions because of human error. Through these patriarchs, God proved His faithfulness to all generations. He created a people who outnumbered the sands on the seashore, just as He promised. He provided for Israel continually. The Israelites erected many stone monuments called "Ebenezers" to remember His miraculous provision.

Throughout Israel's history, He rescued, cared for, provided for, and led Israel with love. He rescued His bride from her suffering in Egypt, led her into the Promised Land, and made her prosper. He created manna from nothing, and when the Israelites thumbed their noses at it, He gave them quail to eat. He fought numerous battles for Israel, making the victory so unlikely that she'd always remember His power. Most importantly, He promised that He could be trusted. He was a husband that would never leave her or abandon her.

Ezekiel 16 explains God's tender provision and care for His bride, Israel:

Then I bathed you and washed off your blood, and I rubbed
fragrant oils into your skin. I gave you expensive clothing of
fine linen and silk, beautifully embroidered, and sandals made of fine goatskin
leather. I gave you lovely jewelry, bracelets,
beautiful necklaces, a ring for your nose, earrings for your ears,
and a lovely crown for your head. And so you were adorned
with gold and silver. Your clothes were made of fine linen and
costly fabric and were beautifully embroidered. You ate the finest foods—choice
flour, honey, and olive oil—and became more beautiful than ever. You looked
like a queen, and so you were!
Your fame soon spread throughout the world because of your
beauty. I dressed you in my splendor and perfected your
beauty, says the Sovereign LORD.
But you thought your fame and beauty were your own. So you
gave yourself as a prostitute to every man who came along.
Your beauty was theirs for the asking. You used the lovely
things I gave you to make shrines for idols, where you played
the prostitute. Unbelievable! How could such a thing ever happen?
You took the very jewels and gold and silver ornaments I had
given you and made statues of men and worshiped them. This
is adultery against me! You used the beautifully embroidered
clothes I gave you to dress your idols. Then you used my special
oil and my incense to worship them. Imagine it! You set before
them as a sacrifice the choice flour, olive oil, and honey I had
given you, says the Sovereign LORD. (9-19, NLT)

The book of Ezekiel was written to the Jewish exiles with Ezekiel in Babylonia. God was judging the Israelites because of their persistent worship of other gods. God had repeatedly warned them through prophets that things wouldn't go well for them if they continued worshiping idols.

When I was reading Hosea from the perspective of the betrayed, I was missing the point of how my own sin grieves God. I can sometimes view things as more important than God, essentially making them an idol. When I choose to make my comfort more important than what God has called me to do, I make comfort an idol. When I worry or focus obsessively on my husband's repentance, instead of trusting God with the outcome of my marriage, I make control an idol. When I believe the lie of culture that says, "Just do what makes you happy. You deserve it," instead of seeking God's will in my life, then I make my self-indulgence an idol.

Comfort, wanting the best for our marriage, and happiness are not bad things in and of themselves, however, when we place these things on the throne of our hearts, they become more important than God. In the pain of processing betrayal, I really began to understand my own sin. Any idolatry in our lives is sinful, and it grieves God, so much so that He describes it as "spiritual adultery."

As I look back over this difficult season of rejection and abandonment in my life, I see God's fingerprints all over it. In the hardest time of my life, God was like a perfectly faithful husband. He walked with me every step of the way, comforting me and loving me. Not once did He desert me, leaving me to flush out the wounds the betrayal had inflicted on my heart.

When my prayers were a constant drip of, "Please help me," He didn't roll His eyes; He listened attentively every time I grumbled about my difficulties. My prayers for help were answered in many ways: comments from my kids that brought me joy, perfectly timed worship songs on the radio that calmed my spirit, and texts of encouragement from friends.

When I used my words to tear my husband down instead of building him up, God gently reminded me to choose my words with self-control and kindness. When I doubted my value, He led me to Romans 5:8: "But God demonstrates His own love for us in this: While we were still sinners, Christ died for us." He reminded me I was worth dying for.

In His love, He didn't force me to choose Him or His way. Instead, when I tried to take control of a situation and finagle it to my taste, He stood by, patiently waiting. He gave me His Word then allowed me to make my own choices, sinful or not. When my plans fell apart, I came running back to Him for help. He forgave me entirely because: "If we are faithless, he remains faithful, for he cannot disown himself" (2 Timothy 2:13).

Throughout Hosea, we get a glimpse of the depth of God's love, commitment, and faithfulness towards His people. (That's all of us!) His love never ceases to pursue the wayward. (That's us, too!) He rescues His people from the slavery of sin. In chapter 3, God sends Hosea to rescue Gomer. He finds her on a slave auction block and buys her freedom. He brings her back home and shows her love, just as the Lord loved the Israelites. Sounds crazy, right?

Hosea had to pay his own money—possibly all that he had—to rescue Gomer from the consequences of her sin. We're not told in Scripture if Hosea hesitated, but verse 2 says, "So I bought her." Hosea saved Gomer.

Like Gomer, each of us has been saved at a cost. Jesus chose to sacrifice His life to redeem us. We have been rescued from the slavery of sin that held us captive.

Here's an important truth I've taken from this journey: Each and every time I sin, I am betraying God. I've realized that I never want to hurt God's heart the way mine was hurt. My desire is to walk this life with faithful obedience, not abandoning my First Love. (That's Him!) I want to love others the way He calls me to. He equips each of us with a desire to obey, a perfect example of love, and grace when we mess up. Even when something else captures our attention and worship,

God's love covers over a multitude of sins (1 Peter 4:8). We can repent by removing the idols within our hearts. In that newly free space, we can ask God to take His seat as Lord of our lives. It's where He desires to be.

I also see God's love from a new perspective. By experiencing the pain of adultery, I came to a greater understanding of God's faithfulness and profoundly experienced His relentless pursuit of me. I was Gomer. Before salvation, I was a runaway idol worshiper. I was guilty of adultery against God, but God was a faithful, loving husband. He rescued me, and He promised to take me back 100 percent of the time. He has a perfect track record of faithfulness. Now, I get to live a life of joy, hope, and peace because of Him.

Prayer for Today

Lord, thank You for being perfectly faithful, even when I am not. Your love amazes me and I never want to hurt Your heart by committing spiritual adultery. Please help me to resist the temptation to make anything or anyone more important than You. The throne of my heart is reserved for You only.

Questions to Ponder

1. In what ways has God rescued, cared for, provided for, and led you like He faithfully did the Israelites?

2. Read 1 Samuel 7:2-12. Samuel erected an Ebenezer between Mizpah and Shen to commemorate how the Lord had helped the Israelites in battle against the Philistines. What practical ways might help you to recall how the Lord has been faithful to you?

3. What are some sins you might need to repent of? Are there areas in your life where you've been spiritually betraying your First Love? Write out a prayer asking for forgiveness.

4. Knowing what it cost Jesus to redeem you from the captivity of sin, how can you thank Him today?

Chapter 20

He's Got a Glorious Future Planned for Me

"For I know the plans I have for you,'
declares the Lord, 'plans to prosper you and not to harm you,
plans to give you hope and a future.'"

Jeremiah 29:11

Go back in time with me to T-minus two days until disclosure, the day after my husband returned from deployment. It was 2 p.m., and my hair was still in the same messy bun I'd woken up with. Our morning hadn't gone as expected.

Will had been gone for 240 days. Usually after he got back from deployment, we'd share a pot of coffee together the following morning, but no one had brewed any that day. The dozen eggs I'd collected from our chickens the day prior lay on the counter untouched. The kids hadn't run into our room and jumped in our queen-size bed for a family cuddle puddle as was customary. The house was quiet, and I was thinking. I'd been awake for most of the night unpacking what Will had said when he'd come home: "I'm not in love with you anymore."

We sat on the porch, watching our three boys play in the front yard. Actually, I was the only one watching. Will was looking at his phone, reading about California divorce law. The kids were out of earshot, and I wanted to talk about the bombshell he'd dropped yesterday. I was confused, scrambled. I needed urgently to sort through the words that had been said. I couldn't take the silence any longer.

"Are we going to church tonight?" I asked.

"Sure," he said.

Will stood up from the rocking chair and jumped off the porch to help our youngest son. Earlier in the day, he'd asked his daddy to take the training wheels off his bike. Will had obliged, but now our son needed him for support for a second lap around the block.

I stayed on the porch and watched them turn the corner. I was disappointed. That had been the fiftieth one-word answer Will had given me all day. Just then, I glanced at my phone and saw an incoming message. It was from Will, a video of our son balancing on the bike all by himself. *Oh my gosh! He's doing it!* I thought, and then an overwhelming wave of sadness hit me.

What if Will and I separated? Was this a glimpse into how we would communicate in the future? Only sharing our kids' keepsake moments through blurry iPhone™ videos? How long before there would be a new woman in the background of the videos? Is that when we'd just stop sending videos all together? Was I going to miss half of my boys' childhoods because our marriage was beyond repair?

Thankfully, we did go to church as a family that night. Being around others who loved Jesus, I felt comfortably at home in their presence. Instead of focusing on the past day's events, my attention was fully fixed on Jesus, the One worthy of all my praise. I don't remember what song lyrics we sang that night, but I praised Him with my arms lifted and my spirit surrendered. Even though my temporal situation hadn't changed, my focus did, and not just for the length of the service.

Going to church that night didn't answer my immediate questions. It didn't provide a shortcut through the mountain in front of me. After worship, a sermon, and a couple of friendly waves, we had a quiet ride home. However, that night I started trusting God more. I knew I needed to release my fear of the future and replace it with the confident assurance of His presence. My marriage was hanging on by a single thread, but I knew my tomorrow was in the hands of the Almighty God. I didn't know what my future held, but I stood firmly on a truth I had heard repeated in my Bible studies: God never wastes our suffering.

Over the last few years, I have seen the Lord faithfully act out the promise of Romans 8:28: "God works for the good of those who love Him, who have been called according to His purpose." I didn't really understand this verse until now. Many times, events and circumstances we suffer through seem pointless and unnecessary, and we can't understand their purpose. The agony of a marriage impacted by betrayal and infidelity is one such circumstance. There is nothing "good" about feeling abandoned and alone, heartbroken and unloved, insecure and afraid. However, my heartbreak drove me to cling to Jesus, my only source of true love, hope, and joy.

Genesis 37-50 recounts the story of Joseph, a man who was driven to cling to the Lord because of his pain and suffering. Joseph's brothers sold him into slavery. He was then wrongfully imprisoned by his former boss. In prison, he was forgotten by the cupbearer who had benefited from his kindness. He spent years in prison because of the selfish choices of his brothers and the perverse lies of Potiphar's wife.

In the dark and lonely moments of confinement—caused by the decisions and actions of others—it was probably difficult for Joseph to make sense of his life. What purpose was there in being a forgotten prisoner? How could any good come from an innocent man serving time as a criminal? However, Genesis repeatedly states that the Lord was with Joseph. I imagine Joseph spent much of his time in prison in prayer and worship. He must have been seeking the heart of God while he waited to be released because he eventually forgave his brothers.

I also assume that as each day passed, he continued trusting God with his tomorrow. In Genesis 50:20, Joseph tells his brothers, "You intended to harm me, but God intended it for good to accomplish what is now being done, the saving of many lives." His heart had been softened and transformed by the hands of the Sovereign Lord. Joseph recognized that there had been a purpose for the years of pain. God hadn't caused the jealousy, the lies, or the selfishness, but He did use the circumstances for His good purpose. Lives were saved, and God's glory was displayed in an act of forgiveness.

As I waited to see what my future would hold, God was softening and transforming my heart step-by-step. Surrendering to the process didn't come easily, and I often tried to take back my perceived control. I would say to myself, *Wow, look how God provided!* Minutes later, I would be forming a new strategy for getting the solution I thought I needed. I would finish praying with a friend, then immediately allow a comment from my husband to steal my peace. The transforming work of the Holy Spirit on my heart was a never-ending process.

During this time of waiting, I often pictured the scenes in Isaiah 29:16 and 64:8 of God as the Potter and myself as the clay. He'd place me on the spinning potter's wheel and begin to mold me into the shape I needed to be in to accomplish the good works He had for me. Ever the resistant lump of mush, I would wiggle out of His hands and fling myself off the wheel to where I thought I should be. He'd patiently place me back on the wheel and start the process again, first softening me with water then smoothing out the rough parts. I'd feel like I was losing my balance as He'd change the rotation speed in order to accomplish His purpose. He'd add a little grog—small pieces of broken pottery—to make me stronger. I'd get offended and warp into something not as beautiful, but He would continue, determined. He'd shave away at the uneven edges, refining my shape again and again.

On this side of Heaven, the refining process is never-ending. There will always be something needing to be surrendered into the Potter's hands. His plans will transform us to reflect Jesus more brightly out into the world. Until we're home, there is always good work to be done in our hearts.

After the betrayal, I wanted my husband to receive the smackdown from the Potter's hands I thought he deserved. Instead, God was working double-time on chipping away at the hardened parts of my heart. The Lord humbled areas of my life where I thought I had it all together. He opened my eyes to my own need for His saving grace.

I remember that not long after D-Day, I was sitting on the beach with my friend, whom I'll call Donna. Will was going to be getting new military orders soon and would have to move. My future was a tangled web of confusion, and I was scared. I told Donna, "I am NOT moving with him."

She cocked her head to the side and said, "I'm sorry?"

"I'm NOT going to move away from my family, my support system, and my church after all of this."

Again, she gently probed, "You're not going to move unless?"

I caught on after that. I sighed, closed my eyes briefly, and finished her sentence. "I'm not going to move unless God tells me to."

Donna smiled at me and, like she always does, reassured me that God always equips us when He asks us to do something difficult. If God had asked me to move, He would no doubt be going with me.

God lessened my anger, softened my heart of resistance, and humbled my pride. I ended up moving with Will. My self-dependence was plucked from hidden areas, and a steady reliance on God began forming. Bitterness and resentment were thrown into the heat to burn, and I slowly discovered true contentment and joy.

God's future plans for me included Him continuing to use disappointments, hurts, and scars to transform my heart. Even now, I still feel like pottery, but more like a piece of Kintsugi—a Japanese art form that repairs shattered works of pottery by both highlighting and gluing the pieces together with gold lacquer at the cracks. The goal of Kintsugi is to showcase the breakage with extravagant beauty, instead of trying to disguise the damage. The repaired piece of pottery is then

151

considered more valuable than it was before. My heart is God's piece of art. The golden scars are proof that my Maker comforts me, heals me, and works for my good in all things (Romans 8:28).

Today, I am living that future I was so unsure of that morning on the porch. I'm more eager to place my fears and anxieties in His hands. I'm more content, and I have peace knowing my future is secure. God has worked for my good and His glory! No day is perfect. My heart is still healing and marital trust is still being earned. Miscommunication and tension in the relationship have the ability to take me right back to that first day. Certain words and images still trigger flashbacks. In all of this, I know God will continue to Kintsugi my heart. I have not arrived yet. There won't be a final product until I am in Heaven. For now, He's given me a desire to comfort you with the truths I've learned about Him on this journey.

I know He can work for your good, too. God didn't cause our husbands to commit adultery. They stepped outside of God's design for marriage of their own volition. They attempted to satisfy their fleshly desires with things that would never fulfill. As daughters of the King, we can echo what Joseph told his brothers, "God intended it for good." Although the process of becoming more like Jesus is a lifelong one, we can be assured that every trial can serve to shape us toward His character. Our future will always be secure. It's in the hands of the Potter.

Prayer for Today

Lord, thank You for not wasting my suffering. I am grateful You can use the hard stuff in life to transform my heart to look more like Yours. Please help me to remember that Your purposes, even though sometimes I misunderstand, are for my good and Your glory. Continue to mold me and shape me as You see fit. I don't need to fear the future when my life is in Your capable hands.

Questions to Ponder

1. In what ways has the Lord used your disappointments, hurts, and scars to transform your heart to become more like His?

2. Jeremiah 29:11 says, "'For I know the plans I have for you,' declares the LORD, 'plans to prosper you and not to harm you, plans to give you hope and a future.'" How does this encourage you when you put it in the context of your current situation?

3. What kind of clay have you been? What kind of clay would you like to be? What kind of finished product do you imagine God making you into? What needs to change in order for God to be able to mold you in that way?

Chapter 21

Putting in
the Hard Work

"See, I am doing a new thing! Now it springs up;
do you not perceive it? I am making a way in the wilderness
and streams in the wasteland."

Isaiah 43:19

Today, I realized finding out about the betrayal in my marriage was actually an act of God's mercy, a miracle, really. It was an unexpected answer to fervent prayers I'd prayed for years. The discovery was the start of something spectacular and was where healing began. I know this might sit uncomfortably with you, but please read on. Give me a chance to explain.

This morning I was reading John 9 as part of my women's Bible study. In this chapter Jesus heals a blind man on the Sabbath. His healing upsets the Pharisees, and Jesus uses the miracle to teach about spiritual blindness. One thing that fascinated me was *how* the blind man was healed. "He spit on the ground, made some mud with the saliva, and put it on the man's eyes" (verse 6). The passage doesn't say the blind man was asking for healing, but Jesus wiped His spit-clay on the man's face regardless. Honestly, it sounded weird and disgusting, until I continued reading.

In verse 38, the ultimate purpose of the bizarre interaction is revealed: the blind man professes his belief in Jesus and worships Him as Lord. Opening the man's eyes was just the start of healing. Jesus had used something gross and dirty to bring physical sight and eternal life to a man who was once blind to both.

Another thing I noticed in this passage was the man wasn't able to see until after he went and washed in the Pool of Siloam. He obeyed, and *then* he was healed. The Gospels recount other miracles in this style. In John 5, Jesus met an invalid man at the pool of Bethesda. Jesus asked him if he wanted to be healed, and when the man confirmed he did, Jesus told him, "Get up! Pick up your mat and walk" (verse 8). Jesus then gave him instructions in order to be healed in his spiritual life, too.

Similarly, in the Book of Mark, Jesus tells a man with a shriveled hand, "Stretch out your hand" (3:5). Another time, when Jesus was teaching, a paralyzed man's friends lowered him down to Jesus through a hole in the roof. When Jesus saw the man, He instructed him to, "Get up, take your mat and go home" (Matthew 9:6b). Jesus told blind Bartimaeus to go, for his faith had healed him (Mark 10:52). Ten men with leprosy were also healed, but only after they headed off to show themselves to the priests like Jesus told them to (Luke 17:14).

When the paralyzed man was instructed to "Get up," I wonder if he was scared of falling flat on his face. How long had it been (if ever!) since he had stood on his own? Maybe he was hesitant, debating if he had heard Jesus' words correctly. Maybe his first few steps were unsteady, not because he wasn't healed, but because he was cautious to put his full weight onto his feet.

What if he had just continued to lay there, never getting up and seeing for himself if the miracle was real? What would be the point of the healing if he had never gotten up and walked? The same goes for the blind man in John 9. After smearing the spit-clay on his eyes, Jesus told him, "Go, wash in the Pool of Siloam" (verse 7). What if the man had stumbled all the way to the pool, only to discover after he washed nothing had changed? He would have risked looking like a fool for

WHO IS GOD NOW?

believing a quack who rubbed spit-clay on his face. But his healing had been at stake. He desperately wanted to get better. He wanted to see! He blindly obeyed and was healed.

The Lord asked me to take some steps of obedience that initially seemed scary. (Don't they always seem that way?) If submitting our lives to Christ in obedience was always pleasant and easy, everyone would be a Christian! Letting go of our perceived control and walking in the unknown is not for the faint of heart. God often asks us to do the hard things that can't be done on our own strength. In turn, these situations cause us to depend solely on Him. It's a process of faith, trust, and growth. When we are faithfully obedient, we get to see how He provides for us and works in our lives. Our trust grows. The next time He asks us to do something difficult, we remember His faithfulness in the past.

For me, opening up to a male counselor about our marital intimacy issues was a step of obedience and a challenge. I had lost trust in all men and read horror stories of women's experiences with Christian marriage counselors. After sharing, the only advice they had received was simply to have more sex with their husbands, as if the affairs were actually the women's fault and having more sex would somehow keep their men loyal.

Our marriage counselor was a retired pastor. Initially, I was humiliated by our situation and embarrassed to discuss it with him, even though he gave sound biblical advice. For months, we met with him weekly on Tuesday afternoons. Somehow, God provided the necessary time off work and childcare we needed to make these sessions, serving to confirm that this was what we needed to be doing.

Compassionate and gentle with my heart, Pastor Dennis was the exact opposite of what I had feared male counselors to be. He showed me he could be trusted and helped me overcome the falsehood that all men are liars. He used humor, not to make light of the situation, but to help us let our guard down. He never chastised me for being overly emotional or for crying. When I wanted to sit quietly, he was patient.

Pastor Dennis supported Will, too. He reminded Will of God's grace and showed him that he wasn't the sum of his mistakes. Will was already ashamed and receiving any more shame, especially from a pastor, would have done more damage than healing. Dennis was truly the mouthpiece of Jesus. He spoke the truth in love and encouraged Will to live in a godly manner.

God used Pastor Dennis to break down the walls of pride and anger in Will's heart, dismantling them brick by brick. After our first session, Dennis offered Will a hug, which Will respectfully declined. By the second month of our sessions, they were embracing like father and son. They even started sitting together during Sunday morning church services. Pastor Dennis eventually saw the fruit of his (and our) hard labor when he officiated our wedding vow renewal ceremony. These uncomfortable months of Will and me being more vulnerable with each other were the spit-clay that helped bring healing to our relationship.

Another step of obedience I took was calling the coordinator of my church's betrayal support group. That call was the first time I had to say out loud that my husband had admitted to numerous affairs and pornography use. Just thinking about the words in my head had made me want to vomit. The feeling only intensified when I considered that this coordinator was a stranger, someone who could very well see me walking my kids into Sunday school the following week. I called though. I asked if she had space, and she welcomed me into the group.

Looking back now, I see that my perception was skewed. The coordinator had the empathy and compassion of someone with a similarly lived experience of betrayal. She was respectful and understanding, but in that moment, I was scared, humiliated. The women in that support group eventually became my closest companions for that season of my life.

We met once a week and prayed. We talked through our frustrations and encouraged each other to choose Godly responses. We prayed some more, studied the Scripture, and acquired tools to strengthen our relationships. I was challenged to implement boundaries in my marriage. I learned doing this was a necessary step towards protecting my heart from further damage. I identified my own denial, passivity, and counterproductive reactions that hindered my healing. I completed difficult journaling assignments that caused me to explore and work through my shock, denial, anger, and fears.

This group was a lot of hard work—work I had to make time for to pursue healing. It was as if I was lying by the pool of Bethesda, like the invalid in John chapter 5, and Jesus was asking, "Well, Robin, do you want to get well?" I did, but I had to get up! I had to make that first phone call. I had to walk into that support group for the first time. I had to share my thoughts about hard topics, read the chapters, and study the Word. I had to write out boundaries and plans, then put them into action when necessary. I had to trust that healing was on the other side of obedience.

I had some fear about writing our story down for people to read. Potentially, some Christian readers will pick apart these words with criticism and judgment. My words might even cause hurt when other women who also trust God don't see the same results that I realized in their marital relationships. I don't know what will happen, but I do know God asked me to write this story. My hope is that these words will help you on your healing journey. On the other side of this difficult obedience is a Father saying to you and me, "Well done, good and faithful servant."

When things were very fresh and I was still hesitant to believe anything good could come from this traumatic experience, I never could have imagined the ways God was going to bring healing into my life. Reflecting on the years since the discovery of the betrayal I can now see how our relationship (mine and Jesus' relationship) has flourished! If the Lord had not opened my eyes to the infidelity happening in my marriage, I would have missed the opportunity of a lifetime: the chance to have my wounds tended to and healed by Jehovah Rapha, the Lord Who Heals. I experienced God in ways I might not have been able to otherwise. As a bonus, I had a backstage pass to witness God's restoration in my husband's life and our marriage.

Our God can bring healing to your heart whether or not your husband ever expresses sincere regret, an apology, or hope for a restored relationship. God's work in your heart is not dependent on any external circumstances. He has everything He needs at His disposal and has been known to heal with only spit and mud!

Prayer for Today

Lord, this is an uphill trek. I want to be an active participant in my healing journey and walk in obedience to You. Please open my eyes to opportunities You have for me. Give me the courage to do the hard things You call me to.

Questions to Ponder

1. As Jesus continues to attend to and heal your broken heart, what is He calling you to do? What instructions is He asking you to obey in order to experience the healing He's offering?

2. Has there been a time when you have obeyed God in a difficult circumstance and experienced a deepening of faith because of it?

3. How does the story of healing in John 9:1-12 bring you hope and encouragement?

Chapter 22

All the Praise Songs I've Ever Learned

"Let the name of the L<small>ORD</small> *be praised, both now and forevermore.*
From the rising of the sun to the place where it sets, the name of the
L<small>ORD</small> *is to be praised."*

Psalm 113:2-3

O ver the past several years, I have been part of an in-depth Bible study. The experience has allowed me to serve alongside amazing Christian women. We're a large group, made up of many smaller groups, one of which I lead. Each week, in addition to leading my own group's Bible study, I have attended a meeting where all the leaders of all the small groups—about fifty of us—have gathered to review the current lesson. In the meetings, we have received tools and guidance for leading group discussion. Over the years, we've asked each other many times for clarity and advice.

One of the most impactful memories I have of this dear group of women was the first end-of-year fellowship I attended with them. At this gathering, a time was purposely set aside for praising the Lord with words of worship and adoration.

It was held in the multipurpose room of the church in which we usually met. We sat on folding chairs in a large circle and chatted with each other as we finished our potluck brunches.

"Time to get started!" announced the teaching leader.

I wasn't sure what to expect, but I followed the cues of the women around me. We tucked the used paper plates under our chairs, then sat on the ground. Almost every woman, with the exception of those in their seventies, bowed towards the cement floor. Their posture was a gesture of humility. They were entering the presence of the King of Kings.

"Lord, we adore You and praise Your holy name," said one woman.

"You are mighty in power," said another.

"You are faithful," said someone to my right.

The women started out by taking turns uttering words of adoration to God. Each would wait until the one currently speaking was done before adding her own praise, but suddenly, the room erupted in a harmony of adoration:

"Omniscient...Worthy of all glory and honor and praise... Light in the darkness... Savior of the world... Prince of Peace... Redeemer."

Even though everyone was speaking at once the words weren't muddled or chaotic. They were harmonious and beautiful, a multigenerational and multicultural hymn of praise. I just sat and listened. My spirit was in awe of God's goodness. I had never experienced something this close to what I imagined Heaven would be like.

When this happened, I had been training with these ladies for several weeks. I was just getting to know some of them. These women had shared their stories during discussion time: one was going through a lawsuit with her next-door neighbor, another was wrestling with the decision to place her husband in a nursing home, and another was grieving the loss of a miscarried grandchild. There was intense pain and grief being experienced by the women in that room. Their faith was being stretched daily by enduring these unimaginable hardships. In the midst of their troubles, they were continuing to worship. Not only that, but they also were exhorting others to do the same. It was awe-inspiring.

As I spent the following years with this group, I began to fashion my own prayer time after the example I saw there. Regardless of the requests I brought before my Father God in prayer, I realized He was first and foremost worthy of my adoration. In my Bible study lessons for this group, the last question of the week was always worded similarly: "What attribute of God stood out to you in this lesson?" or "What did you learn this week about the character of God that you can praise Him for?" I had previously answered these questions with a cursory word or two, but over time, I started looking deeper for answers. In what new ways could I praise God? After all, the whole reason I studied His Word daily was to know Him better.

When I learned a new truth or an old truth was revealed in a fresh way, I shared it with my sons. I didn't want their knowledge of God to be limited simply because of their vocabulary. They loved learning God is an Avenger. He is just, fair, and will avenge His people. God's a real superhero. It's biblical!

My boys and I began a new bedtime routine we called "Praising God's Attributes," in which we told each other whatever attributes of God we wanted to highlight that night. The most fun was when their cousins slept over. Sometimes our praise would become us belting out the lyrics of whatever worship song was popular at the time. There's nothing like rock-band-style worship to help settle in five boys at a slumber party. Witnessing our boys as the up-and-coming generation of Christian men praising God made my sister and me joyful. Our boys proclaimed God to be their "Miracle Worker, Healer, Avenger, and the One Who Saved Baby Moses from Getting Dead."

Currently, my boys are growing in maturity and faith. Our Praising God's Attributes practice is sometimes still interrupted by bodily noises and fits of giggles, but the truth of God's character is sinking in. The other night, after I tucked the kids in, I turned on the TV and started watching an impassioned Bible teacher lecturing on Ephesians. My middle son heard the woman's loud voice and came downstairs. He looked at the TV.

"Can you please turn that down?" he said. "I thought it was you yelling at someone on the phone, and I prayed for God to give you peace."

My nine-year-old knows in his soul that true peace can only come from Jesus, the Prince of Peace. (I'm still not sure why he assumed I was yelling at someone, but such is life with kids.)

We have watched the Lord work constantly in our lives. My boys recognized God as Healer when their uncle received a double lung transplant to save his life. They saw him as the Giver of Perfect Peace when we prayed after they awoke from nightmares. We celebrated Him as Emmanuel at Christmas time and Risen Savior at Easter. God showed up as Abba Father during their dad's lengthy deployments, and they understood Him as the God of Grace when they needed to ask for forgiveness. He was the God of Compassion as we prayed that their great grandma, who was suffering from dementia, felt His love. They asked Him to be their Comforter when they had to move away from their home, school, friends and family in California.

The truth is, I hope my boys are learning from me the same eternal truth I learned from the Bible study leaders on that day of adoration: God is praiseworthy no matter what. He is worthy because of who He is, not because of what He does or doesn't do. We can praise Him even when He isn't answering our prayers the way we want or within the time period for which we hoped. He deserves all honor and praise because He alone is holy.

Praising God in difficult times doesn't always come naturally or easily. There were many times after D-Day I didn't understand what God was doing. I couldn't see a way towards restoration or even the slightest glimmer of hope.

"Why God?" I would ask. "How could You allow this to happen?"

I couldn't discern an answer.

"God, can you give me a direction, maybe a neon sign with an arrow pointing the way?" I would pray.

"Be still and wait," I could hear Him say in my spirit. Sometimes, He would simply say, "No."

"God, please make this suffering stop. Make my pain go away. Just give me relief!" I would say.

"Not yet," He would respond.

Why did He give me the answers He did? Perhaps it was because He was doing a good work in me. Maybe through my suffering He was producing greater endurance, character, and hope. Perhaps He was preparing my heart to write these words to you. What I know to be true from my experience is that no matter how He is handling the situation with you and your husband, He is perfectly good at being our Perfect God.

One tool I've found particularly helpful on my healing journey is reciting God's praiseworthy attributes in alphabetical order. When I read a passage of Scripture that contains a new (to me) attribute of God, I note it on the piece of scrap paper I keep at the front of my Bible. It's worn at the edges and creased down the middle, but I treasure it. I never want to forget who God is and what He has done. That paper represents at least five years' worth of character discoveries. All the letters of the alphabet are written vertically down the page. Next to each letter, in miniscule handwriting, I've written descriptions of God that start with that letter.

Here's a few of my favorites from my "A," "B," and "C" sections. (You can read the complete list at the back of the book.)

A. Avenger (2 Samuel 22:48; Romans 12:19), Abba Father (Romans 8:15), and God of Abundance (2 Corinthians 9:8; Ephesians 3:20)

B. The Bread of Life (John 6:35), Binder of Wounds (Psalm 147:3), and Bridegroom (Matthew 9:15)

C. Constant Companion (Joshua 1:9), Comforter (2 Corinthians 1:3-4), and Compassionate (Exodus 34:6; Psalm 145:8)

The only one I've found for "Z" is Zion's King (Psalm 48:2), and I don't have any for "X." (If you find one, please let me know!)

All of these attributes are reasons to praise Him. The truths we learn about Him as we study His Word can transform our thinking and ignite passionate praise. I challenge you to make your own list. It doesn't have to be in alphabetical order (that's just for us Type A people). We can praise Him any time we learn something new about Him. As we meditate on God's Word, we become more intimate with Him. Our attitude of praise becomes a lifestyle. Author Marian Jordan Ellis said it beautifully: "If we are filled with the Holy Spirit, the proof pours forth in praise."[3]

Paul gives us the perfect example of praising God despite one's circumstances. He penned a long list of his devastating experiences, which might not even have been all-inclusive or comprehensive, in 2 Corinthians 11:23b-28:

> *I have worked much harder, been in prison more frequently, been flogged more severely, and been exposed to death again and again. Five times I received from the Jews the forty lashes minus one. Three times I was beaten with rods, once I was pelted with stones, three times I was shipwrecked, I*

---

[3] Marian Jordan Ellis. For His Glory: Living as God's Masterpiece. Nashville: Abingdon Women, 2020. 163. ©2020 Abingdon Press Used by Permission. All rights reserved.

spent a night and a day in the open sea, I have been constantly on the move. I have been in danger from rivers, in danger from bandits, in danger from my fellow Jews, in danger from Gentiles; in danger in the city, in danger in the country, in danger at sea; and in danger from false believers. I have labored and toiled and have often gone without sleep; I have known hunger and thirst and have often gone without food; I have been cold and naked. Besides everything else, I face daily the pressure of my concern for all the churches.

One time, Paul and his traveling companion, Silas, cast a spirit out of a fortune-telling slave girl. Her incensed owners had them stripped, severely beaten, and thrown into prison. Night fell, and even with their feet fastened in stocks and their wounds still seeping blood, they mustered the strength to praise God. They prayed and sang hymns, and the other prisoners began to listen (Acts 16:16-40).

Do you sometimes feel like Paul with your heart beaten up so badly it doesn't seem like it will ever heal? Do you feel like your circumstances have put you in a prison of depression, your feet fastened by the chains of fear and anxiety? I definitely did while processing Will's betrayal, but I was inspired by Paul and Silas. I encourage you not to leave the biblical lesson in biblical times. While working through the injustice of infidelity, when my heart—through no fault of my own—had been crushed and pounded, I was challenged to ask myself, how could I give praise to God through it?

Within a month of finding out about my husband's infidelity, summer turned to fall, and it was time for my Bible study group to start meeting again. As the day of the first meeting approached, my insecurities began to creep in. In my leadership role, I wanted to rejoice with women who were rejoicing and weep with women who were weeping. I couldn't see how I could point people to Jesus when my heart hadn't even begun to heal yet. How could I shepherd women when I might soon be walking through a divorce? I was tired—physically, emotionally, and mentally. I could try to put on a happy face each Wednesday. Maybe I would be able to hold back my tears, even as they threatened to overflow from my eyelids. I honestly felt I didn't have much I could give.

After weighing these thoughts, I decided (not God!) what I needed to do was to step down from leadership. I called my teaching leader and briefly explained the situation. I told her I needed to take a break from my role as a Bible study leader. Her response shocked me.

"You're not going to step down from your role," she said. "You are going to continue to serve through this trial. There's no better time to choose to praise Him than through the storm."

At first, I thought she was being totally unsympathetic, but, as we continued talking, she assured me the best possible place for me to be was within my circle of faithful Christians. She told me they would help me to praise God through the worst of trials, that they would lead me by example, and they did.

If you are considering stepping down from a role you know God has called you to, I want to encourage you to seek His will before you decide what to do. Your husband's addiction, his behavior, and your broken marriage does not define you. Your divorce doesn't label you. You are not imprisoned by your circumstance. None of those things take away the truth that you were created to glorify God. You didn't lose your purpose when your husband cheated on you. Don't let your circumstances dictate whether or not you'll continue to serve or praise God. Paul and Silas didn't!

Even after Paul and Silas were released from prison, they continued to travel, share the gospel message, and love others well. Find yourself a Silas, a companion who will walk through the tough times with you, reminding you of God's goodness. God is always praiseworthy and deserving of honor and glory, not just when life feels good. Let's be women who, when persecuted and unjustly treated, can be heard praying and singing to God, just like Paul and Silas.

When we praise God for who He is, we can ignite a chain reaction of praise. There's a story in Acts 3 of a lame man who was sitting at the temple gate, begging for money. As the apostles Peter and John walked by him, Peter said to the man, "Silver or gold I do not have, but what I do have I give you. In the name of Jesus Christ of Nazareth, walk" (verse 6). In a miraculous healing, the Lord strengthened the man's body instantly. Ligaments and tendons that hadn't ever supported muscles or bone before became strong. Atrophied muscles began bearing weight. The Bible says that the man jumped to his feet (verse 8). His legs hadn't worked for his entire life, and now he could not only stand, but jump. The man knew it was a miracle of God.

"When all the people saw him walking and praising God, they recognized him as the same man who used to sit begging at the temple gate called Beautiful, and they were filled with wonder and amazement at what had happened to him" (verses 9-10). What we can glean from this man's experience is that he didn't hide the miracle. He wasn't scared that, for some reason, his legs might not work the following day. He responded immediately by praising God in the temple courts.

As the Lord heals our hearts from the devastation of betrayal—and He will—we can praise Him throughout the process. We know there was never any hope of us bolstering ourselves after this tragedy. The Lord has performed miracles in our hearts and lives. This is why we're able to stand. Furthermore, He will continue these works. As we consider who God is, what He's capable of, and what we've seen Him do so far, we can show our gratitude with praise. Others will recognize us as the women who were once betrayed, but now walk in an attitude of praise. He deserves all the glory.

Prayer for Today

Lord, it hasn't been easy to have an attitude of praise when my life has been turned upside down. I know You are worthy of all glory, honor, and worship. Please help focus my mind on Your attributes. Open my eyes to the many reasons I have to praise You.

Questions to Ponder

1. In what ways has the betrayal impacted your desire or willingness to praise God?

2. What thought patterns might be interrupted if you recognized God as deserving of praise, no matter what?

3. Start your own ABC attribute list. What are some things you can praise God for right now? Where do you see His character working in your life today?

Chapter 23

So Where Does This Leave Me?

"Though the fig tree does not bud
and there are no grapes on the vines,
though the olive crop fails
and the fields produce no food,
though there are no sheep in the pen
and no cattle in the stalls,
*yet I will rejoice in the L*ORD*,*
I will be joyful in God my Savior."

Habakkuk 3:17-18

While D-Day didn't end World War II, it laid the foundations for the Allies' future victory. On the evening of June 6, 1944, their triumph still seemed a long way off. In fact, mothers were expectantly waiting to learn the fate of their own sons' lives. Soldiers were begging their comrades to hold on until help would arrive, and countless wives were suddenly widows. Even though it would take until the spring of 1945 for the Nazis to be defeated, D-Day turned the tide for the war. Suddenly, there was a spark of hope. That day, General Eisenhower encouraged Americans that even though much fighting remained, victory was on the horizon. The Allies could—and would—win the war.

I didn't know it on my D-Day, but God had a glorious victory planned for Will and me, though like the Allies, our victory was a ways off and required hard work to accomplish. Will and I attended separate betrayal groups once a week. He met with a psychologist. My mentors challenged me to pray for Will daily. We formed new habits of communication and made our expectations clear. We wrote down things we liked about each other and ways we enjoyed spending time together.

We actively sought out ways to love the other person well. Thought patterns needed to be rewired and rehearsed. Boundaries were put in place and consequences were agreed upon. Homework assignments had to be completed for weekly marriage counseling sessions. We read books and listened to helpful podcasts. We began, for the first time in our marriage, to read devotionals and pray together. A plan of action and accountability needed to be addressed before each work trip. We also began new routines for both our own relationship and our time as a family of five. All of this work stemmed from getting our hearts in the right place with God.

I may never understand how God prompted my husband to disclose his betrayals that day. He tells me he had always intended to take his secrets to his grave. While our rejuvenated marriage is amazing, what is more amazing is looking back and seeing all the ways God has worked in our lives. To God be the glory! It's only because of His power, His grace, His love, and His unwavering commitment to finding the best in His creation that we were able to rebuild a beautiful marriage from the ashes of our old one.

My story of betrayal did not have a predictable ending. Many others have confirmed this with their unsolicited comments: "I would have left him," "I could never stay," and "There's no way my husband and I could ever stay together in a situation like that." Maybe these statements reflect your current reality more than my story. Some of you may be living out your worst-case scenarios as you read this. Perhaps you've tried and tried, but have recently realized your partnership is beyond reconciliation. Maybe your husband has already moved in with someone else and started a new family. Maybe he's so far down the path of alcoholism or drug abuse that you can no longer communicate clearly to each other. No matter the details, I grieve with you. There is nothing right, nothing fair, nothing okay about any of this.

Even as you walk through this war zone, God is with you. He does not leave His children alone to flounder in the wreckage of a broken marriage. He remains with you, and He is your peace (Ephesians 2:14). I pray this book has provided you with a spark of hope and the confidence that you will be victorious.

Betrayal does not have the final say. God will get you through this.

Let me say it again: God *will* get you through this! Perhaps with a repentant husband. Perhaps not. Ultimately, the person most changed by your husband's betrayal will be you. Don't let roots of bitterness spring up and choke out the goodness God is showering over you. As your faith grows, your fear can subside. As you lean into Jesus to provide, your anger can lessen. Your heart can soften as you read and meditate on His Word. He reveals Himself to those who diligently seek Him. As you become better acquainted with His character, your trust in Him will become unwavering. You can hold firmly to the hope of your future victory. It won't be easy, but it will be worth it.

Who is God now? God hasn't changed, my friend. He's the same all-powerful, all-knowing Father He was before you and I were betrayed; and He will continue to be. It's His character.

My Prayer for You

Lord, thank You that in Your kindness and love, You've placed this book into this woman's hands. As she navigates her journey to overcome betrayal, please assure her that she can place her hope and trust in You. Shower her with the comfort, peace, and joy You perfectly provide. May she be encouraged to invite You on her healing journey.

Questions to Ponder

1. What's the most meaningful truth you've discovered about God? Which truth has been the most challenging to believe?

2. How have your perceptions of God changed? How have your responses to Him changed in light of what you now know?

3. Why is it important to keep your hope in God when your heart's been betrayed? What steps can you take to grow in your relationship with God?

4. How can you take what you've learned and share it with other women who need this message?

Acknowledgements

To my husband, thank you for fighting the hard fight. Every. Single. Day.

To my wise mentors Judy, Diane, and Kelley, thank you for spurring me on in the faith, challenging me with hard questions, and speaking the truth in love. I want to be like you when I grow up.

Lynne, thank you for modeling reverence to the King of Kings, teaching me about God's attributes year after year, and for encouraging me to not give up serving.

Diane, thank you for making sure that my writing remained biblically accurate and honorable to my husband.

Rachel and Nicole, thank you for just listening.

Dennis, I'm glad you convinced my husband he can be a hugger.

To my family, thank you for loving the two of us through our worst time. You remained non-judgmental, and I'm forever grateful for your love and support.

Thank you to my sister, Christy, for your encouragement to tell of God's glory. You are the best companion writer and motivator I could ask for. You're kind of funny, too. Look what He's done!

Sticky Note
Love Notes

Truth about God's Love for Me Based on Scripture

He has loved me with an everlasting love. Jeremiah 31:3	God's love has been poured out into my heart through the Holy Spirit. Romans 5:5	How priceless is Your unfailing love, O God. Psalm 36:7
Because of the Lord's great love, I am not consumed. Lamentations 3:22	God lavishes His love on me and calls me His child. 1 John 3:1	Nothing in all of creation will ever be able to separate me from the love of God. Romans 8:39
Perfect love casts out fear. 1 John 4:18	God showed me His great love by sending Christ to die for me while I was still a sinner. Romans 5:8	For God so loved me that He gave His only Son. John 3:16

May I have the power to grasp how wide and long and high and deep is the love of Christ. Ephesians 3:18	I will be glad and rejoice in Your unfailing love, for You have seen my troubles and You care about the anguish of my soul. Psalm 31:7	Give thanks to the God of heaven. His love endures forever. Psalm 136:26
In His love, He no longer rebukes me. Zephaniah 3:17	Because of His great love for me, I am saved. Ephesians 2:4-5	He keeps His covenant love to a thousand generations. Deuteronomy 7:9
My God abounds in love and faithfulness. Psalm 86:15	His unfailing love for me will not be shaken. Isaiah 54:10	God showed His love for me by sending His Son into the world. 1 John 4:9

God's Names and Attributes

Note to readers: This is not an exhaustive list. I encourage you to start your own and add to it as you learn more about who the Bible says God is.

A. Advocate (1 John 2:1), Atoning Sacrifice (Romans 3:25), Avenger (2 Samuel 22:48; Romans 12:19), Alpha and Omega (Revelation 1:8; 22:13), Abba Father (Romans 8:15), Ancient of Days (Daniel 7:9), Abounding in Love (1 John 4:7-11; Psalm 103:8-12), Awesome (Deuteronomy 10:17; Psalm 68:35), God Almighty (Genesis 17:1; Psalm 80:19; Revelation 1:8) You Answer Me (1 John 5:14-15), and God of Abundance (2 Corinthians 9:8; Ephesians 3:20)

B. Bright Morning Star (Revelation 22:16), the Bread of Life (John 6:35), Bridegroom (Matthew 9:15), Blameless (2 Samuel 22:26), Beginning and the End (Revelation 22:13), and Binder of Wounds (Psalm 147:3)

C. Creator of Heaven and Earth (Genesis 1:1; 14:22), Constant Companion (Joshua 1:9), Close Friend (John 15:15), Comforter (2 Corinthians 1:3-4), Chief Cornerstone (Ephesians 2:20), Compassionate (Exodus 34:6; Psalm 145:8), Chooses Me (Ephesians 1:4), Clothed with Splendor and Majesty (Psalm 104:1), Coverer of Sins (Romans 4:7-8), and Counselor (Psalm 32:8; Isaiah 9:6)

D. Deliverer (2 Samuel 22:2; Psalm 37:40; 56:13), Drives Out Fear (1 John 4:18), Dominion Endures from Generation to Generation (Daniel 4:3), Delights in Those Who Fear Him (Psalm 147:11), Destroyer of the Devil's Work (1 John 3:8), My Delight (Psalm 37:4), and My Defense (Exodus 15:2)

E. Encourager (Romans 15:5), Exalted (Psalm 57:5), Eternal (Exodus 15:18; Job 36:26), and Everlasting (Isaiah 40:28; Psalm 90:2)

F. Friend (John 15:13), Firm Foundation (Isaiah 28:16), Faithful and True (Revelation 19:11), Faithful in All He does (Psalm 145:13), the First and the Last (Revelation 1:17), He Will Not Forsake Me (Psalm 37:28), He First Loved Us (1 John 4:19), Father of Heavenly Lights (James 1:17), Forgiver (Hebrews 8:12), He Is for Us (Romans 8:31), My Fortress (Psalm 46:7; 2 Samuel 22:2), Firstborn from the Dead (Colossians 1:18; Revelation 1:5), Forerunner (Hebrews 6:20), and Full of Grace and Truth (John 1:14)

G. Gracious Giver (Romans 8:32), Glorious (Psalm 145:5, 12), Giver of the Spirit (Romans 8:11), Good Shepherd (John 10:14), Greater Than He Who Is in the World (1 John 4:4), Great King (Psalm 95:3), God of Abraham, Isaac, and Jacob (Exodus 3:6), Guide (Psalm 23:3), Great God (Deuteronomy 10:17), Giver of Wisdom (James 1:5), Good (Psalm 145:9), and God of Gods (Deuteronomy 10:17)

H. He Holds Me (Psalm 139:10), Holy (Isaiah 57:15), My Hiding Place (Psalm 32:7), My Helper (Hebrews 13:6), Healer of Broken Hearts (Psalm 147:3), Horn of My Salvation (2 Samuel 22:3; Psalm 18:2), My Hope (Hebrews 6:19; Psalm 37:34), High Priest (Hebrews 5:10), Healer (Psalm 30:2), Holds My Life in His Hands (John 10:28-29), and He Hears Me (Psalm 55:17)

I. I AM (Exodus 3:14), Immanuel (Matthew 1:23), Intercedes for Us in Prayer (Romans 8:26-27, 34), Instructor (Matthew 23:10), and Immortal and Invisible (1 Timothy 1:17)

J. Just (1 John 1:9), My Joy (John 15:11), Judge (James 4:12), God of Jacob (Psalm 146:5), He Justifies (Romans 8:33), and Jealous (2 Corinthians 11:2)

K. King of Kings (Revelation 19:16), King Eternal (1 Timothy 1:17), Kinsman Redeemer (Ruth 1-4), and King of Glory (Psalm 24:8)

L. Light of the World (John 8:12), Love (1 John 4:8, 16), Lord My God (Psalm 25:1), Lord of Lords (Deuteronomy 10:17), Lawgiver (James 4:12), Laid Down His Life (1 John 3:16), Lamb of God (John 1:29), Lives in Me (Galatians 2:20), Living One (Revelation 1:18), My Lamp (2 Samuel 22:29), and Lord of Kings (Daniel 2:47)

M. Makes Everything New (Revelation 21:5), Maker of Heaven and Earth (Psalm 146:6), Merciful (Ephesians 2:4), Master (Luke 5:5), Messiah (John 4:25-26), Mighty Warrior Who Saves (Zephaniah 3:17), Most High (Genesis 14:18, 14:22; Psalm 57:2), Mighty God (Isaiah 9:6), Mighty in Power (Psalm 147:5), Majestic Glory (2 Peter 1:17), Majestic (Psalm 29:4), Majesty (Hebrews 1:3), and Our Mediator (1 Timothy 2:5)

N. He Is Near (Psalm 145:18)

O. Overcomer of the World (John 16:33), One Who Sees Me (Genesis 16:13), Omniscient (Isaiah 46:9-10), Omnipotent (Deuteronomy 10:17; Ephesians 3:20), Omnipresent (Jeremiah 23:23-24), and Owns All Wisdom and Power (Job 12:13)

P. Protector (Psalm 32:7), Provider (Philippians 4:19), Promise keeper (Psalm 145:13), Perfect (Matthew 5:48), Praiseworthy (Psalm 148), God of Peace (1 Corinthians 14:33), Pure (2 Samuel 22:27), Preserver of My Life (Psalm 119:25, 138:7), Preeminent (Colossians 1:18), and Prince of Peace (Isaiah 9:6)

Q. Quick to Help (Psalm 18:6-10)

R. My Rock (2 Samuel 22:2-3; Isaiah 26:4), Rescuer (Psalm 55:18), Refuge (2 Samuel 22:3; Psalm 57:1), Redeemer (Galatians 4:5), Radiant (Psalm 76:4), Refresher of My Soul (Psalm 23:3), Righteous in All of His ways (Psalm 145:17), Ruler of Kings of the Earth (Revelation 1:5), Restorer (Psalm 80:19; 1 Peter 5:10), Reviver (Psalm 80:18), Robed in Majesty (Psalm 93:1), Revealer of Mysteries (Daniel 2:47), He Reigns (Psalm 93:1), the Rock That Is Higher Than I (Psalm 61:2), Raised to Life (Romans 8:34), and Rich in Love (Psalm 145:8)

S. Savior (2 Samuel 22:3; Psalm 55:16), My Strength (Exodus 15:2), Sustainer (Psalm 55:22; Isaiah 46:4), Security (Hebrews 6:19), Salvation (Exodus 15:2), Sovereign Lord (Genesis 15:2; Jeremiah 32:17; Romans 8:28), Our Perfect Sacrifice (Hebrews 10:14), Shield (Genesis 15:1; 2 Samuel 22:3; Psalm 3:3), Stronghold (2 Samuel 22:3; Psalm 37:39), Shines His Face on Me (Numbers 6:25), Shepherd (Psalm 23:1), Son of Man (John 3:13), Sits Enthroned (Psalm 29:10), Sufficient (2 Corinthians 12:9), Spirit of Truth (John 16:13), My Safety (Psalm 27:5), Shuts the Mouths of Lions (Daniel 6:22), a Sun and Shield (Psalm 84:11), Satisfies Me (Isaiah 58:11), and Slow to Anger (Exodus 34:6; Psalm 145:8)

T. True God (1 John 5:20), Triumphant (Colossians 2:15), Trustworthy (Psalm 145:13), the Truth (John 14:6), Tower of Strength (Proverbs 18:10), Teacher (Matthew 23:8), the Lord Is There (Ezekiel 48:35), and True Light (John 1:9)

U. Upright (Psalm 25:8; Isaiah 26:7), Upholds the Righteous (Psalm 37:17), Unfailing Love (Psalm 32:10), Unchanging (Psalm 55:19), and His Understanding Has No Limit (Psalm 147:5)

V. Victorious (Deuteronomy 20:4), True Vine (John 15:1), Vindicator (Psalm 57:2), and Our Very Great Reward (Genesis 15:1)

W. Faithful Witness (Revelation 1:5), With Me Forever (Joshua 1:9), Wonderful Counselor (Isaiah 9:6), Worthy of Praise (Psalm 145:3), Way, Truth, and Life (John 14:6), Watches Over All Who Love Him (Psalm 145:20), Who Is, Who Was, and Who Is to Come (Revelation 1:4), Without Sin (2 Corinthians 5:21), and the Word (John 1:1)

Z. Zion's King (Psalm 48:2)

About
Kharis Publishing:

Kharis Publishing, an imprint of Kharis Media LLC, is a leading Christian and inspirational book publisher based in Aurora, Chicago metropolitan area, Illinois. Kharis' dual mission is to give voice to under-represented writers (including women and first-time authors) and equip orphans in developing countries with literacy tools. That is why, for each book sold, the publisher channels some of the proceeds into providing books and computers for orphanages in developing countries so that these kids may learn to read, dream, and grow. For a limited time, Kharis Publishing is accepting unsolicited queries for nonfiction (Christian, self-help, memoirs, business, health and wellness) from qualified leaders, professionals, pastors, and ministers. Learn more at: https://kharispublishing.com/

Milton Keynes UK
Ingram Content Group UK Ltd.
UKHW020712091024
2079UKWH00001B/3